Live Again Our Mission Past

by

Barbara Linse, Educator and Author

George Kuska, AIA, California Architect

Art Direction/Production .... Ken Gillespie
Art Direction/Production Updating .... Richard Judd
Mission Sketches.. George Kuska
Drawings .... Cynthia D. Clark
Young Authors .... James Byrnes and Sherry Miller

New

Original Hispanic California Stories
for Kids to Read in English and Spanish
(20 pages)

Published by

ART'S PUBLICATIONS

80 Piedmont Court, Larkspur, CA 94939

415-924-2633

Distributed by

EDUCATIONAL BOOK DISTRIBUTORS

P. O. Box 551, San Mateo, CA 94401

FAX 415-344-7840

Second Edition - 1984 / Third Edition - 1992 / Fourth Edition - 1996

Eleventh Printing - 1996

Library of Congress No. 83 -072050

ISBN 1-878079-11-5

This edition has been approved
by the California State Department of Education
[illegible]ce

About the Authors

arbara Linse has a B. A. in Education and a General Elementary Teaching Credential from California State University at San Jose and an M. A. in Education with credentials in Supervision and Administration from California State University at San Francisco. She has spent two years of advanced graduate work in the School of Education at Stanford University and two years in Mexico studying Latin American cultures.

Ms. Linse taught fourth and fifth grades for five years and was a general elementary and art consultant for the Monterey County, California Office of Education and supervised Elementary student teachers for San Francisco State University for four years. She has spent fifteen years teaching extension and summer sesssions in elementary school art and social studies. These classes have been in-service education classes in California school districts.

Ms. Linse is the author of three Fearon-Pitman pulbications : *Well-Seasoned Holiday Art, Elementary Art Activities* and *Arts and Crafts for All Seasons.* She co-authored *Papier Maché* for Sunset Publishers and for MacMillan, wrote six art education films for children. She wrote *The Art of the Mexican Folk* and co-authored *Live Again Our Mission Past,* published by Arts' Publications. Co-authored *Love the Earth,* an ecology book for young children. Also, a teacher resource book, *Put On A Circus.*

orge Kuska graduated in 1947 from the University of Nebraska's College of Arts and Science with a degree in Architecture. In 1948 he received a B. A. from the College of Engineering, fulfilling his fifth year for national acceptance as an architect.

Mr. Kuska designed the Tower of the University of Nebraska and has designed numerous schools, churches and libraries in San Benito, Fresno and Monterey Counties.

He is the past president of the Salinas Rotary Club and Chamber of Commerce and is the past president of the Monterey county Chapter of the American Institue of Architecture.

He served on the Salinas Planning Commission and Design Review Board for eight years each and on the Salinas Board of the Boy Scouts of America from 1957 until the present.

George Kuska is from Kansas and began his career in Salinas. He found himself surrounded by the Carmel, Soledad, San Juan Bautista, San Antonio de Padua and Santa Cruz Missions. His background in architecture heightened his fascination and study of these wonderful buildings.

If you might like a teaching workshop focusing on the Missions or Mexican Folk Art for youngsters, please contact: **Barbara Linse**
ART'S Publications, 80 Piedmont Court
Larkspur, CA 94939 (415) 924-2633

(These workshops are for teachers, parents or other adult groups.)

Table of Contents

Page

Exploring California

Columbus discovered the New World in 1492. By the early 15 hundreds Spain owned much of it including Arizona, New Mexico, Texas, Baja and Alta California. In 1542 the King of Spain, the Viceroy of Mexico and everybody else thought Alta California was an island. The king called a Spanish soldier, Juan Rodriguez Cabrillo, to check it out.

A Native California woman told Cabrillo. "Your clothes are different, aren't they? You don't understand me? You don't talk as we do."

Exploracion California

Colón descubrió el Nuevo Mundo en 1492. Ya al principio del siglo dieciseis España controlaba gran parte de estos nuevos territorios entre ellos Arizona, Nuevo México, Texas, Baja y Alta California. En 1542 el rey de España, el virrey de México y todos los demás pensaban que California era una isla. El rey llamó a un soldado español, Juan Rodríguez Cabrillo para que lo comparbara.

Una indígena californiana le dijo a Cabrillo, "Su ropa es distinta a la nuestra, ¿a que sí? ¿No me comprende? No habla como nosotros."

Acknowledgments

We express our thanks to those of you at each mission who made this revision possible. Our most enthusiastic appreciation is to each member of the California Mission Studies Association who has given friendship, papers, tours and hospitality. It is largely through this membership that the missions are living again.

We thank everyone who helped us with each edition of **Live Again Our Mission Past** book.

Our special thanks go to those of you at each mission who made this edition possible.

We appreciate the generosity and enthusiasm of those administrators of the Oakland Museum and the California State Parks System *(Sonoma Region Office)* who made possible, our photographs taken on their presmises. Likewise, we appreciate the fine assistance of *Susan Vignes Hahn* of the University of San Francisco.

The California State Park System *(Sacramento Region)* provided direction and descriptions for such topics as Indian Games, Bartering, Adobe, Candle and Soap Making. Our California State Park System and the Oakland Museum are top resources for parents, teachers and children.

Our thanks go to Chapman College and Mission San Juan Capistrano for such liberal use of their archeological finding, and to *Kristie Butterwick* for her charming mural at that Mission.

A very special thanks is given to the children who are photographed popping from pots, dipping candles, rubbing noses with donkeys, weaving on the big looms and engaging in other activities of that early era. *Michelle* and *Wayne de Fremery, Ross* and *Hadyn Murray, Amy* and *Mickey Lippett,* thanks. *Tony* and *Carrie Watts,* a special thanks to you. You two were shot so often it's great you are still alive!

We thank those talented fourth graders in *Ruthe Linblums's* class at Dixie School District who illustrated the *Calexto Legend.* Hooray for *Bill Dittman,* owner of the Marin Teacher's Store, who observed that this book is needed in the homes and schools of California. And thanks, *Aunt Margaret!*

Most especially we thank those valiant fourth grade teachers who interrupted their programs to make special Mission Murals. It was important to have the Story Boards and Dioramas which were done in the classrooms of *Claire Mosconi* and *Marita Randolph* of Neil Cummins School. To Mrs. Meister of Saint Anselm's School, we thank you for that Saturday morning in June when we photographed your fourth graders' Missions.

Our special thanks go to those of you at each mission who made this edition possible.The real fourth grade teacher of this book is *Mary Beth Forrest* of Hoover School in Palo Alto. For two years we visited her classroom frequently as her youngsters shared Native American ideas; Mission and Ranchos, and even let us pan a little gold. *Serri Miller* and *Larisa Carpo* were both from *Mary Beth's* classroom.

We have enjoyed the collections of mission memorabilia and Native American artifacts.

Native North American Artifacts

Dedication

We dedicate this book with affection to the natives who first lived in California. May we hold our state in the high esteem and treasure her resources as did the Natives who first lived here. Throughout our text we call these people Native Californians, Native Americans and Indians.

Columbus thought he was going to the East Indies when he discovered this new world so he named all of the native peoples "Indians."

Barbara Linse

Introduction

Live Again Our Mission Past is presented to help each of the California Missions gain new life.

You, as parents, teachers and other participants, are encouraged to use it fully. Become introduced to earlier times through the Acorn-Nut Shell summaries; make copies of the plays for simple or more complicated enactment, and the Legend of Calexto for everyone's fun and a clearer understanding of the two Californias, Baja and Alta, and their similarities and differences.

The beautiful Mission drawings would be very nice in any home or classroom, and the recipes in any kitchen. The activities are meant to create and permit a clearer understanding of the life during these times through simulation or participation. The Haul of Records is for bits and pieces, great and small. The history-geography gives a sound background of the time and place.

Some people may read through the book; some may start at the middle and read their way to either end. Others may go from the end to the beginning and some may play hopscotch, going hither and thither.

Enjoy the special resources for the various missions: plan to paint on the blacktop at Santa Barbara– or share the Living History days at Sonoma or La Purisima Missions – as Native Americans lived and worked together.

This is a book with something special for every California Mission enthusiast. Those among you who teach are invited to photocopy anything for distribution within your classroom.

We invite you to join us in this adventure. Dip a candle. Have a fiesta. Visit a Mission. Read a legend. There is lots of fun waiting for you.

A Child's Story

Living With California Indians

James Brymes

Indian children worked hard but they had time for fun too. They played games like hockey. The players had curved wooden sticks and a wooden ball. Another game was hoop and pole. The hoop was rolled on the ground and they would try to throw a pole through the hoop. Basketball was played and tug of war. They liked guessing games and a game like "Button, Button" and dice games played with walnut shells. They would bet on these games and sometimes lose their homes and food.

Girls had dolls and cradles and boys had small bows and arrows. They also played a game like hopscotch and hide and seek.

There were lots of children in the village because everyone lived together. Boys and girls could wander from family to family and live with a second set of parents. They could stay with them and sleep with them.

Indian children wore clothes made of hides. In the winter they wore clothes on top of each other for warmth. Women made the clothing.

Children learned by doing. They learned from their parents and hunters. Girls learned to treat leather for clothes and how to take care of babies.

Boys were given tests for bravery.

Indian children had a hard life compared to our life today. When the white men came to the Indian lands they made their life even harder by taking their land and bringing white man's diseases.

Boys and girls learned never to cry out loud. They might give their position away to an enemy or scare animals.

Indian children learned by making mistakes. They were not told that fire burned. They

learned by burning their fingers.
When a boy was ten, he was expected to hunt
On his first hunt he couldnt keep any of the food for himself. He had to share it with everyone.
When a boy was 12 he had to go to the mountains far away by himself with no food for 4 days.

Indians believed everything had a spirit.

A Sample of Native American (Jauneño) and English Terms

by Etta Rommel, San Juan Capistrano Museum

Some suggestions for the pronunciation of Harrington's transcription are as follows:
h kl m n p s t v w y are pronounced approximately as in English.

The consonant X is the fricative sound of German ch in Bach or of Spanish j in José.

The nasal consonant n is like English ng in singer.

Accent falls on next-to-last syllable, unless otherwise indicated

Vowels, a, e, i, o, u, have approximately the same values as in Spanish vaca, Pepe, shico, toro, luna.

S is like s in sin

The spelling tc represents the sound of English ch as in chin

English	Ajachme
Misc.	
Indian shelter	kiitca; puki'
rock	toota
shell (mollusk)	layl
water	paala
river	wanitc
Indians	'ataaxum
The Reverend	Rivirentu
arrow	huula
church	wamkitc
Animals	
black bear	hunwut
brush rabbit	toovet
mountain lion	tukwut
valley coyote	'ano''
Birds	
duck	qaatqat
ducks	qaataqtum

English	Ajachme
Birds (cont.)	
goose	la'lam
owls	kukuulum
bald eagle	paamuS
golden eagle	aSwut
roadrunner	puy'puy
condor	yunaavaywut
Insects	
ant	'aanat
tarantula wasp	pu'ulakic
black widow	ku'xinic
Food	
acorn mush	wiwtc
blackberry	pilula
fish	anammat
Colors	
red	qwayaqwyac
green	malomluc
blue	kunoknuc

In an Acorn Shell

The Native Californians affected by the California Missions were dwellers along the coast and inland to fifty miles or so, from San Diego to Sonoma. Though these people were from twenty-seven separate tribes, they shared a good life with one another. Their land yielded a bounty of good things. They didn't have to travel far for food and shelter. Each tribe spoke a different language. When the Native Californians lived together in the Missions they were taught Spanish.

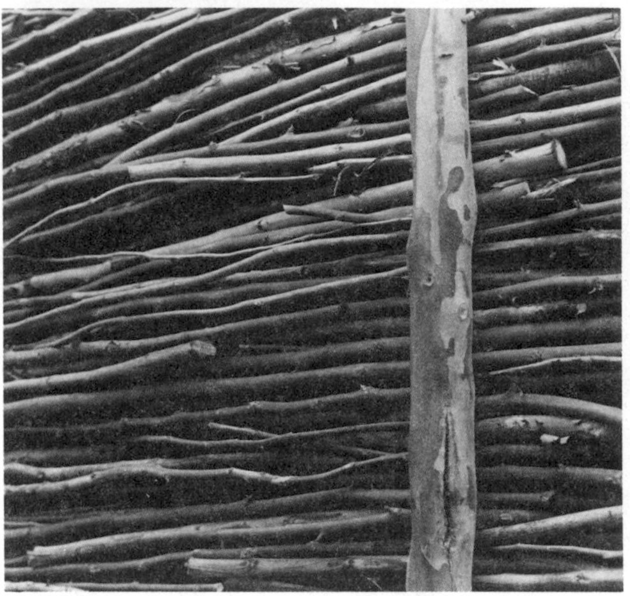

These coastal Indians, though living in separate tribes, shared many things Their economy was based on hunting and collecting. They had similar topics for myths, legends, and folktales.

Food was plentiful and included; from the tide-lands, shellfish, and surf fish; acorns from six or seven oak species; salmon and trout from the ocean area; buckeyes, pinenuts, lake and river fish, and land mammals from the foothills. The climate was so mild that the land was like an ever-changing menu with various nuts, berries, blossoms and fruit ripening at about the same time each year. Acorns, leached and ground, provided a real food staple. The land yielded the goods for home dwellings. Thatched tule and willows were used as weather indicated, and as they were available. In moderate to cold weather tule was used. Shelter from cold and rain was provided by the use of thicker thatch. Bundles of willows or wood were used also.

Baskets and pots were made and used, and these generally warm, accepting people had time to decorate them. Mortars and pestles were made and used for grinding acorns. Shoes were made of rush or leather. Fur robes were used in winter, and tule mats were very nice for the floor covering. Babies were diapered in rich, soft moss.

Musical instruments played a real role in the life of the tribes. Pebbles in cocoon rattles, bird bone whistles and elderberry flutes were among the instruments creatively fashioned.

Clam disk beads, *(as shown)*; stone or wood tobacco pipes; a multitude of herbs for medicine; carved arrow heads; soap stone for washing; cooking vessels and bird bone earrings were among the materials used by these Native Californians.

The Native Californians played some games that will be listed and described here. The "game time" only constituted a portion of their week's activities. It was to this happy atmosphere that the Spanish came.

The achievements of these coastal California Natives were great. They fashioned many styles of boats for fishing and travel. They used materials around them for making mortars and pestles, weapons and tools. Some Native Californians had regular lumber mills. The ingenuity of these early inhabitants is to be admired. Both women and men made everything. They had snow shoes, redwood stools, pipes, grinding rocks and granite frying pans.

The Native Americans were pantheistic in their religious views, and believed that all plants and animals were as alive as human beings. They had completed accounts of the world's creation. They differed from the Spanish Catholics in believing that nature was filled with divinity.

The California Natives had customs, languages and religious beliefs which varied from group to group. These were intelligently developed over time.

Food was quite plentiful, but real inventiveness was shown in the ways which women, girls and boys gathered food, hunted and fished. Trees were usually cut down by building a fire at the base, applying wet mud, and forcing the fire to burn right through the trunk. The tree was then pushed or pulled down.

Beautiful duck decoys, very special baby cradles, quail traps and nooses for hunting were among the objects made and used in everyday life. Some Native American groups made raised beds, others made deer sandals. In summary, there was a richness and diversity in the life styles of early California Natives.

Among those customs widely practiced in California were purifying one's self before a hunt, and giving thanks for food supplies.

Time Line

	1542	1602	1769
California	The Indians were hunting and gathering food; leaching acorns; making dwellings from wood or tules; and catching fish or jumping into the sweat house.		
Spanish Explorers	Cabrillo explored and died in Alta California	Viscaino traveled up the coast and turned back	First actual settling in California

They would first gather tule leaves Then they dried them. And then they made a frame
Then they stitched the sides of the house. They made the sides out of willow poles.
Then they put up the stitched sides over the frame.
Inside the house, they dug holes in the ground for the beds and a hole in the roof for the

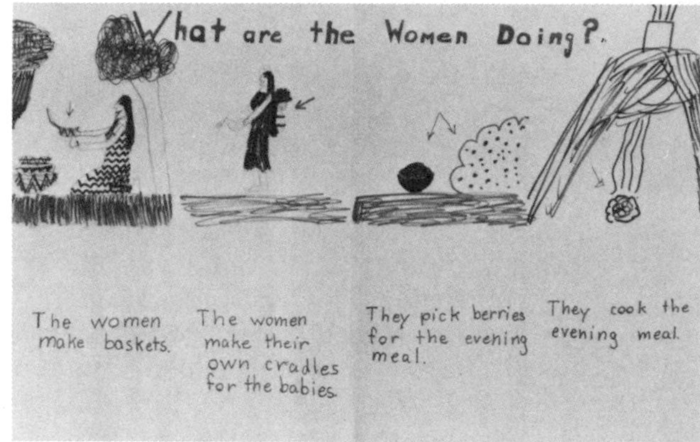

What are the Women Doing?
The women make baskets.
The women make their own cradles for the babies.
They pick berries for the evening meal.
They cook the evening meal.

Then they take all the seeds off with a split wooden stick.
Then they weave the dry weeds. They also put red and black in the baskets.
The baskets are finished. It took many days until it was done.

The men first walk to the steam room
They start a fire in the fire pit
They wipe the sweat off them with split deer ribs.
When the men can't stand the heat any longer they jump in the lake, river, pond, etc.

The Legend of Calexto: the Make-Believe Maker of Alta and Baja California

Calexto was the Creator God of California and was so bold and selfish that the other gods didn't want him around. He was so pleased with his first creation that he didn't want to share it. He shouted to the east that Alta California was an island *(it wasn't! See map - page 47)*, so that he could keep it for himself and his most precious Indians.

He gave them many wonderful things; food and beauty from the sea, streams of fresh water and a nice climate. There were plenty of seeds and berries for the Native Californians to eat, hills to protect them from the wind, wood and willows to build shelters, and reeds for making baskets tight enough to carry water, and to cook fish and meat. There were round rocks for grinding acorn meal and other things. In fact, Calexto was so good to the Alta California Natives that many of them had beautiful rabbit fur coats and moss with which to diaper their babies.

When Calexto saw how beautiful his Alta California was, he was afraid that newcomers might come from the south and take it from him, so he decided to make Baja California a barrier to keep them out. This god would create a land that would tempt people to come, but would be difficult and challenging enough so that they would have to work hard to live there, and would stay away from his precious Alta California.

When he heard that explorers had discovered the new world of which the Californias were a part, he said, "I must keep the California Island Story alive so that those snoopers won't come and take away this beautiful land." So Calexto shouted it again, "Alta California is an island!" and the wind carried his voice into the right listening ears.

The explorers stayed away from Alta California. Calexto caused trouble in Mexico to keep Cortés busy, and dropped pearls in the bay at La Paz to keep the attention of explorers on Baja California. Cabrillo might have spread the word about Alta California, but while he was still in Baja, Calexto had pushed him into the yerba flecha, an herb that causes temporary blindness, which caused him to fall in San Diego, break his arm, and die of the infection. His log books, recording all he had seen

until his death in Santa Bárbara, were sent to the King of Spain.

Later, the travels of Viscaino brought another threat to Calexto's plans. There were now many doubts about the island story, and Calexto didn't want anyone to get close to Alta California. When Viscaino was coming along the coast, Calexto sent a big fog to cover some of the best harbors, so that Viscaino wrote in his log that someone else should look at it again.

When the Jesuit priests decided to bring Catholicism to the Indians of Baja California, Calexto wanted to make sure they wouldn't go farther north.

"This is the Mexico you know," Calexto whispered to the wind. "Look what happened to your brothers in Alta California, Cabrillo and Viscaino. One died and the other was fogged out."

The kind Jesuit Fathers heard these whispers as they went about their work in Baja California. It was close to Mexico, and after all, wasn't Alta California possibly an island? Didn't bad things happen to everyone who tried to explore it? "The Indians here need our help," the fathers said. "They can't even get enough food."

The King of Spain got a message or two telling of pools of pearls and mountains of silver in Baja. Do you suppose Calexto sent the words?

The priests wanted to help these poor, hungry Native Americans get more from the meager land, and Calexto wanted to keep them away from Alta California. He got the native folks and Spaniards to work together building the first chapel of palm thatch, and then, when the heat got to him, Calexto left them working and went to Alta California to enjoy the delicious food and good climate.

Back in Baja California, Calexto decided to reward the hard working people by giving them some good things. He created the wild fig, zalati, which grows in crevices of rock, and the organ cactus, which bears a nectar-like fruit for two full months in the

summer. He added tiny snapdragons, popcorn flowers and lots of palm trees; these had no fruit, but gave promise of better things to come.

So the people worked harder and harder to stay in Baja, where the land was beautiful, but rain and food were scarce. Despite the difficulties, the first Mission was built at Loreto, on the coast, with large rocks and mortar. Between 1697 and 1768, twenty Missions were built in Baja California. Calexto's great plans were succeeding.

But perhaps Calexto was becoming too smug and self-satisfied. He would take long naps after his big meals, and, while he was sleeping, Spain was making plans that would ruin Calexto's private paradise forever.

The Jesuits left Baja, and the Franciscans came for a year. When Portola and Father Serra traveled to San Diego to start the first Mission in Alta California, Calexto sent storms to delay the ships, and tried to stop the land travelers with hunger and disease. By now Calexto's powers, along with his muscles, were getting weak, and this time he could not keep the travelers away.

Once the first settlement was begun, there was nothing Calexto could do to keep California to himself. News of the wonderful climate and pleasant land spread to the rest of the world, and Calexto found himself helpless to prevent people from coming in and making California into one of the most important and beautiful states in a new nation.

And what happened to Calexto, who had made the land for himself and then had to watch it taken over by strangers? No one really knows, but some people say that when he saw the first buildings going up at San Diego, he ran down from the hills and jumped into the sea, causing a gigantic splash. And even now, people say, when the great whales travel slowly along the coast of California, Calexto might be out there with them, forever looking back at the beautiful land he created and lost.

In a Nut Shell

THE BAJA CALIFORNIA INTERVAL

The peninsula of Baja California became the focus of Spanish interest. Stories were told of silver mountains and lakes filled with pearls. During the sixteenth century, Cabrillo, Viscaino, and others had explored the hot, dry, and rather barren land. After Cortez spent a year near the present site of La Paz, Spain decided to have Baja settled by missionaries. In 1697, the Jesuits started the first Mission and colonies, which were easily reached from Mexico across the Gulf of California.

Twenty Jesuit Missions were founded, with great difficulty, in the next seventy years. *(See Great Haul of Records).* Rain was so scarce that almost nothing grew, and the native people were killed in large numbers by the epidemics which were brought by the Spanish and to which the natives had no natural immunity.

The Mission system was an inexpensive way to colonize a land and its peoples. In the Californias, the priests could build with native materials and could use the food of the land to supplement their diet. Practical crafts were taught to the Native Americans, and goods were produced in Mission workshops that could be used by the settlement or in trade. Many needed supplies were brought to the Baja Missions, principally from the Far East.

Mission locations were selected where water was accessible, and where crops and animal fodder could be grown. While the primary goal of missionaries was to Christianize the natives, they also hoped to establish communities where women, men, girls and boys could engage in agriculture.

Despite effort and planning, the Missions in Baja California did not prosper. The land, though pleasant in winter, was too rocky, too dry, and too

hot to encourage settlement. In 1768, the Jesuits' twenty Missions were transferred to the Franciscans and Father Junipero Serra came to Baja as their president.

In the following year, the king of Spain and the Viceroy of Mexico, rereading the notes of Cabrillo and Viscaino describing the green grass and golden flowers of Alta California, ordered Serra to leave the Baja Missions and join Governor Portola's expedition to the north and to establish a Mission at San Diego. This was to be the first of many built in Alta California.

Exploring California

A play to be read together by a group of people, probably children.

The play can be divided into the sections of your choice.

Masks and puppets can do the talking.

Costumes and scenery are not necessary, imaginations will do.

Write your own play in your own ways. Feel free to photocopy *(as shown on title page).*

SCENE I – 1542

Cast – Storytellers *(can have several)*

Cabrillo

Sailor

Indians

Possible props – Pictures of old maps

Notebook for ship's log

Storyteller 1

The year is 1542. It was thought that California was an island. Spain owned all of Mexico including, of course, Baja California. Juan Rodriguez Cabrillo, a Portugese explorer, was called on by the King of Spain and the Viceroy, Spain's representative of Mexico, to check out this so called island of Alta California.

Storyteller 2 *(reads a poem for this occasion)*

The Viceroy of Mexico
Said, "Up, Cabrillo, and off you go,
You can have ships and folks of all sorts.
Please bring us back some good reports
of Indians and silver and gold.
The very thought just makes me feel bold!
Claim all this wealth in the name of Spain's King
And around the world your praise we'll sing!"
The year was 1542.
I'm glad they discovered our land, aren't you?

Storyteller 1 *(continuing)* – He sailed past the west coasts of mainland Mexico and Baja California and eventually landed at the spot where San Diego harbor now lies. Cabrillo and his men were ready for a good rest.

Cabrillo – This is such a beautiful spot. Look at the green grass and golden flowers. *(Looking at the Indians)* Don't you understand? Don't you speak Spanish? We will name this spot for Saint Didacus and claim it for Spain. San Diego, that's its name. I must get this all down on my maps and in the ship's log *(Cabrillo picks up map and ship's log).*

Native California Woman *(to Cabrillo)* – Your clothes are different, aren't they? You don't understnad me? You don't talk as we do.

Storyteller 1 – After some days of rest and a pleasant time on shore with the Native Americans, Cabrillo and his men and his little boats went on up the coast. They saw smoke on the shore! Was something cooking? Was it cold? They called it "The Bay of Smokes."

Storyteller 2 – This could have been Santa Monica or, perhaps, San Pedro. Cabrillo had put into many ports to get food, so his crew got very little scurvy. They had fresh berries to eat. Cabrillo and his men sailed to Santa Bárbara's Channel Islands. They always had little gifts for the Indians, like necklaces and other trinkets.

Cabrillo — We'll call these islands the Santa Bárbara Islands and the land nearby Santa Bárbara. Whoops, I'm falling *(Cabrillo falls on his arm).*

Sailor — He's broken his arm, I think. *(turning to Cabrillo)* Be careful, sir! *(Cabrillo exits. He reappears with a sling around his arm)*

Storyteller 1 — The men sailed up the coast of California. They passed *(big sigh)* Monterey Bay and San Francisco. . . . .

Storyteller 2 — But they never really saw the harbors. Maybe it was because these harbors were all fogged in. *(to audience)* What do you think? Soon after, Cabrillo got really sick, because his arm became infected and he died.

SCENE II — 1602

Use new storytellers — *(they can be daughters and sons of other storytellers).*

Cast – Storytellers

Viceroy

Viceroy's Aide

Viscaino

3 Sailors

3 Native Californians

Possible props — An hourglass

A clock

A telescope *(use a paper cylinder)*

3 small ships

Paper for log keeping

Storyteller 2 — The year is 1602. The new Viceroy of Mexico was pacing back and forth in his office in Mexico.

Viceroy — We have to do something about Alta California. They say it's an island, you know?

Aide — This new Señor of the sea might be of great help. They say that he is brave and true and never gives up, and he's very good at keeping his ship's log — and we do need someone who writes because there aren't a lot of explorers or anyone else who writes these days, or reads either.

Storyteller 2 — In May of Sixteen Hundred and Two,
Not having anything else to do,
Said a later Mexican Viceroy
"Viscaino, you're quite a boy!
You can have three ships, that's quite a few.
An explorer's life is waiting for you.
From San Diego, please go on North,
And see what the harbors and land are worth.
From Acapulco, sail up the shore,
I don't believe it will be a bore!

Storyteller 1 — They sailed off from Acapulco on May 5, 1602.

Storyteller 2 — Sebastian Viscaino, the explorer, had his trusty hour glass *(and a minute minder, too)*, clocks, telescopes, two hundred men, three small ships and lots of paper for log keeping. He was full of courage.

Storyteller 1 — On November 10, 1602, San Diego was spotted. It had a beautiful natural harbor. The sailors and Viscaino went ashore with happy faces and empty tummies.

Sailor 1 — Ahoy, there. We are here!

Storyteller 2 — Of course, it was said in Spanish.

Sailor 2 — I feel so sick, could it be scurvy?

Sailor 3 — The what?

Sailor 1 — Scurvy, scurvy! You often get it on ships.

(Note: Maybe some of you children can look up scurvy and bring the cure back to 1602)

Native Californian 1 – Have some acorn mush and clear water from the stream.

Sailor 3 — I wonder what they are saying. Oh, look! Food. I'll try anything. Wow! It's so good!

Viscaino *(writing in his log)* — The natives are wearing rabbit fur capes and deer skin wraparounds.

Storyteller 2 — After some days together, they said their goodbyes to the Indians in Spanish.

Sailors *(as they wave goodbye and leave in their canoes)* — Adios, amigos.

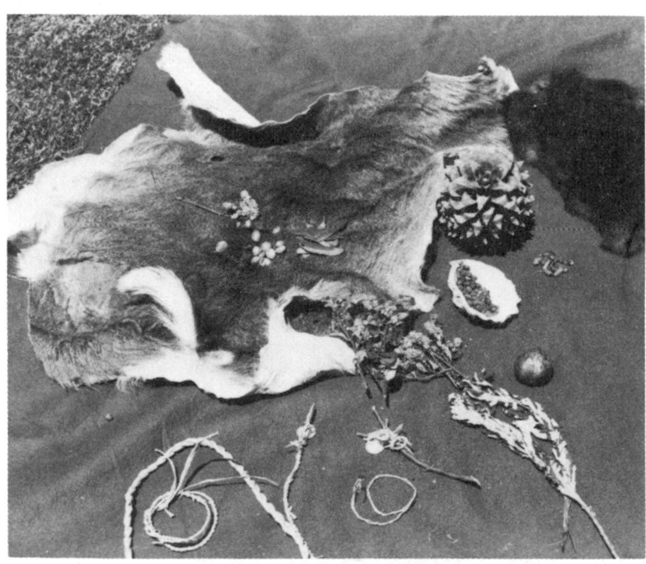

Native Californian 1 – What are they saying?

Native Californian 2 – They are going.

Native Californian 3 – Look at their hands going up and down in the air. They mean "goodbye."

Storyteller 2 — They sailed on and on . . . . . all three ships.

Viscaino *(with a telescope – paper rolls)* — This must be the harbor we read about in Juan Rodriguez Cabrillo's log.

Storyteller 1 — Viscaino wrote about the green grass and golden flowers in the log. He also wrote of stopping at Monterey Harbor, which he described as a sheltered bay with a fine port. He told of white oaks, and live oaks, and fresh water and hills. As they sailed north from Monterey, they sailed past San Francisco Bay, for it was covered by a blanket of fog. The party returned to Mexico and turned in the log to the Viceroy who sent it to the King. It stayed with each successive king until 1769, when the then King of Spain re-read the accounts and decided to settle Alta California. The word was out that the Russians were coming into this land, and it certainly had been proven that it was not an island.

Storyteller 2 — Why didn't anyone go back for 167 years after this?
(Children in the class can respond with these and with their own answers.)

1. I guess the trip was too hard, and the explorers must have said so.
2. They couldn't carry enough fresh water, and ocean water is too salty.
3. They couldn't take very good food on the ship. It was all salted or dried, but never fresh.
4. It would have taken too much room or gotten rotten if they had taken fresh food.
5. The trip was hard because they never knew how hard the winds would blow against them and how long the trip would take.
6. Lots of people got scurvy, and that's no fun.
7. That's because they didn't have any food to eat with enough Vitamin C, as found in lemons, limes, oranges, grapefruit, and a little bit in most every fruit or vegetable, and even in the brown husks of rice.

Exploring California

The group sailed off from Acapulco on May 5, 1602.

Sebastian Viscaino, the explorer, used an hour glass and a clock to keep track of time, two hundred men, three small ships and lots of paper for his ship's log.

On November 10, 1602 they saw San Diego. It had a beautiful natural harbor. The sailors and Viscaino went ashore with happy faces and empty tummies.

The following are remarks which might have been in Viscaino's log: "The natives are wearing rabbit fur and deer skins. They gave us acorn mush and clear water from a stream. We can not understand them. They do not speak Spanish.

Exploracion California

El grupo zarpó de Acapulco el 5 de mayo de 1602.

Sebastian Viscaino, el explorador, utilizó un reloj de arena y otro reloj normal para medir el tiempo. Iba acompañado de doscientos hombres, tres barcos pequeños y mucho papel para el diario de navegación.

El 10 de noviembre de 1602 vieron San Diego. Tenía un precioso puerto natural. Los marineros y Viscaino desembarcaron con cara de felicidad y los estómagos vacíos.

Puede que Viscaino haya escrito lo siguiente en su diario de navegación: "Los indígenas llevan pieles de conejo y cuero de venado. Nos dieron gachas de bellotas y agua clara de un arroyo. No los entendemos. No hablan español."

The 1769 Play
The Franciscans Come to Start the Missions

Cast — Storytellers
Alexandra
King Carlos of Spain
King's Aide
Father Junipero Serra
Jose de Galvez
Gaspar de Portola
Sailor
Captain
Missionary
Doctor Pedro Pratt
Blacksmith
Father Crespi
Captain Rivera

Alexandra — I am Alexandra, I was born in Russia. We have found fine seal furs in Alaska for the hard Russian winters. We moved down here to Alta California. *(speaking to the storyteller)* Did you hear?

Storyteller 1 — Oh yes, and so did the King of Spain.

(office of the King of Spain)

King Carlos — If we are to own the world, we better get busy with Alta (Upper) California. We have certainly had a bad time with Baja (Lower) California. Spanish settlers don't like the desert, so Alta California suits them fine.

Aide – Oh but, your majesty, the Franciscan Brothers are doing their best in Baja California. The Missions that they work in are nice, but the weather is so hot; the ground is very hard and rocky; the crops will not grow; and the Native Californians are not interested in becoming "neophytes." That's what the Franciscan Brothers call their converted native people.

Storyteller 2 – Yes, that's the story. The reasons California, Baja and Alta, were settled were to Christianize the Native Californians and to hold the land for Spain from Russian and other European countries.

King Carlos — The Russians are in Alaska, and some are in Alta California already. I say we take all of the Franciscans out of Baja California and send them to San Diego. *(He turns to his secretary with a long quill pen and commands)* Write to my man in Mexico, Viceroy Jose de Galvez, and tell him to go to Alta California and start building Missions up the coast. They can hold the land for Spain that way and Christianize the Indians all at the same time.

Storyteller 1 — Well, Galvez got the letter. He went to the town of Loreto, the capital of Baja, and told the plan to Gaspar de Portola, the governor, and Father Junipero Serra, the Mission president.

Father Junipero Serra — We can work with the Indians and help them become Christians and farmers and speak and read Spanish. In about ten years we can leave a group of them, and they will be good farmers.

Storyteller 2 — They both wanted to help people get on their own feet.

Jose De Galvez — Portola shall stay long enough to establish Monterey, but Father Serra will be head of all the missions and stay until they are all built.

King Carlos *(reading from the diaries of Cabrillo and Viscaino)* — These early explorers talk about green grass and yellow flowers in Alta California, and of friendly Indians. I hope we find success.

(Loreto, Baja California)

Father Junipero Serra and Governor of California, Gaspar De Portola *(singing)* —
We'll start some towns in Alta California
To hold the lands and Christianize the folk.
We'll send two ships a-sailing to San Diego.
The rest of us will walk, and that's no joke.

Father Serra — I hold the position
That we should start with a Mission
And build it with materials around.
With these books on architecture
I won't attend a lecture.
We'll make adobe bricks with sand and ground.
(Some straw for sticking but the main ingredients are sand and clay.)

(Mexico)

(Large group of people gathered in front of a ship and sailors ready to go to San Diego on the first ship)

Sailor — Captain, I'm a sailor on this ship, I guess.

Captain — Well, if you're a sailor on this ship you will have twenty-four shipmates who are sailors. This fine vessel is the *San Carlos*, and we're off to start the town and Mission of San Diego.

Missionary *(calling out with dignity)* — Excuse me, excuse me. I'm a missionary. May I get on the ship?

Blacksmith — And I am a blacksmith. May I get on the ship?

Captain *(carrying ship's log book)* — Will you please jot down that the *San Carlos* sailed from Baja California on January 9, 1769?

Sailor — Yes, sir.

Storyteller 1 — Excuse me. There are some things our audience needs to know. The *San Carlos* took one hundred and ten days to get to San Diego, and most of the people were sick with scurvy because they did a foolish thing and took only dried foods to eat. Also, the ship *San Antonio* left a month later and took only fifty-five days at sea. Then the land parties started out . . . Let's watch the land parties get started.

(on the way to California)

Father Crespi – Captain Rivera, do you think that twenty-five soldiers are enough to take along? Remember, we'll be taking cows, some bulls, horses, mules, tools, food and seed on the mules, and lots of Native Americans.

Captain Rivera – Oh, Father Crespi, that will be plenty, but I am really counting on you to keep the official diary. I hear you're the best.

Portola – We'll be leaving in few days. I'll be with Father Serra and Sergeant Ortega. We'll have animals and soldiers and Native Californians. Be sure, all of you, to find nice grassy places with fresh water for camping. You'll need grass for the animals, you know, and we will carry some water in leather containers. We will also take the architecture books.

Father Serra *(writing in his journal)* — I had a very bad sore on my leg. The muleteer put some wild herbs on it. My sore is getting a lot better now. There are roses everywhere, and I have been eating berries and even grapes in the canyons. It is so beautiful here.

Doctor Pratt — I am Pedro Pratt and I shave Father Serra daily.

Father Serra — This does look like Cabrillo and Viscaino's description of San Diego. Where are the ships?

Storyteller 2 — We are out to finish the play, six months after starting, all four groups are here together in San Diego.

(San Diego)

Father Serra *(hanging a bell on a tree)* — San Diego. We have made it. I can't walk very well, but life is so good, and I am so happy.

Storyteller 1 — The next three Mission sites were selected because of their harbors, fresh water source and position against the mountains. The remaining seventeen Missions in the chain were founded so that they would be only a day apart by horse or on foot.

Note: The days of departure to San Diego:

January 7, 1769 — the *San Carlos* sailed and the trip took about one hundred and ten days.
Early February 1769 — the *San Antonio* departed and arrived in San Diego seventy days later.

Father Crespi, the good diary keeper, and Captain Rivera's land group left on **Good Friday 1769**. They had one hundred and eighty mules and five-hundred domestic animals and many Indians who died or left the group on the way north. They arrived two months later.

Captain Portola and Father Serra left in **mid-May 1769** and arrived on **July 1**.

EPILOGUE TO THE PLAY

A group of padres and Indians were sitting around a fire at Mission San Carlos in Carmel *(This could be dramatized as Father Serra tells the story, or it could be read in parts.)*
Father Serra — Did you hear about Portola finding Monterey? *(everyone shakes head "no.")* — He was told by the king to find Monterey Bay. You see, Viscaino had written all about this beautiful spot. Well, Portola started off with a small group of men with all of Senor Viscaino's records and went searching for Monterey. They got here but they didn't recognize the shore and another nearby. He felt so bad that he didn't find Monterey Bay *(even though they had)* that he went back to San Diego.

Another Priest — Tell the part about the mules.

Father Serra — Do I have to? Well, all right. The men were so sad and hungry and sick on the way home that they ate their mules to stay alive. I know that to be true. They all smelled like mules — through this very nose *(points to nose)*. When Governor Portola took another land group back to the site of the cross he followed on the *San Antonio*. The cross was right by the harbor all decorated by the Indians with meat, shellfish, feathers and arrows stuck in the earth and with a string of sardines. On June 3, 1770, bells were hung. All of the people came in their very best clothes and the Mission was blessed. We all began to build the Mission and the presidio of Carmel and Monterey right here. I'll never forget the big cannon roll that was like thunder that came right after the dedication on this very spot.

Mission Plans in Alta California

The Viceroy of Mexico told Father Serra: *"You will be head of a new Mission system – at each there will be a church, workshops, small houses, crops, and classes in Spanish and religion."* Crops will be planted; sheep and cattle raised; weaving and basketry, ceramics made for own use; tallow rendering and skin drying which will be used for trade; a chapel for worship; and the buildings and occupants will all be part of the Mission. As soon as the Mission was functioning, the priests would leave and start another Mission.

This ideal included:

- having all the buildings complete and well-equipped kitchens with enough wood stoves and ovens;
- food for preparation, all raised at the Mission;
- Mission craft rooms for self-sufficiency;
- big looms for weaving, and spinning wheels, brought from Boston, for rugs, blankets, and clothing;
- clay for making pots, although most of the pots, dishes and utensils were brought from Mexico and were used for cooking and serving.
- basketry making for gathering, carrying, and storing all sorts of foods;
- adobe making, for new bricks and for building and replacing old bricks.

Sleeping quarters were to have been finished and furnished. Some were not, even when secularization took place. Classrooms were built for teaching religion, and speaking and reading Spanish. Farming skills were to have been mastered, as well as the techniques of candle dipping, tallow rendering and hide drying. The chapel was to have been complete as religion was an intrinsic part of each day. The plans didn't always work. Why? The Native Californians came from the stone age and had so much to learn. For example, it was difficult to teach them to read because of the tremendous intervention of epidemics, earthquakes, Native Californian raids, and pirateering, all of which was unforseen. Priests, Native Americans and townspeople worked together from the Mission's beginning to the time of secularization.

Education – The Native Americans were taught Spanish. This was the most practical language to use because of the number of Native American dialects.

because of the number of Native American dialects.
Certainly the Spanish had to learn some native dialects. They had problems to solve and probably all learned together. It was not possible to teach all of the Native Americans to read, however, because they were so busy.

Here are some thoughts about the basic needs of the Spanish and Native American people:

- where are the Native Americans now, in a land that had been theirs for generations? They had lived here for centuries.
- how did the Spanish and Mexican and Native Californians get along?
- what was the *climate* like for the Spanish settlers?
  The climate of California is like that of Spain. Both areas have Mediterranean climates.
- what changes in *culture* had to be made for both groups?
  As you look through the *food* recipes see who had to make changes.
- what changes took place in *clothing*?
  The Native Americans expanded their wardrobe with sheep and wool.
  What else might have happened?
- what type *shelters* were available?
  The Spanish started with Native American types, and changed to adobe and tiles.

Safety – Had there been earthquakes all through the centuries? It's not safe for anyone to be in an adobe brick Mission in an earthquake.

Epidemics – The Spanish colonizers unknowingly brought highly contagious diseases to the Native Americans. the Europeans and Mexicans had built up immunity by contact to such maladies as smallpox and measles. The Native Americans, on the other hand, had no previous contact with such sicknesses; had no immunity and, consequently, were killed in vast numbers on their initial contact with the diseases.

Disease and Its Effect on Survivors –
As disease was rampant, many children were left seriously incapacitated and crippled. We can look with admiration at these children and adults, Native Americans and Spanish-Americans, who overcame their handicaps and led such very useful lives.

In an Acorn Shell

MISSIONING IN ALTA CALIFORNIA

The orders arrived from Spain. Father Serra was to take people and supplies from Baja to Alta California to found Mission San Diego de Alcalá. Three ships and two land parties set forth on journeys of from three to seven months. Those on the walking trip took with them most of the Mission livestock, including horses, cows, chickens, and sheep. Soldiers and townspeople from Baja came along to found a city and presidio in San Diego. Hunger, scurvy and exhaustion made the trip difficult and caused some deaths along the way.

Two ships, *San Antonio* and *San Carlos,* arrived safely, but a third vessel, *San José*, sank with its cargo of food and supplies needed at the Mission. The cargo included 10,000 pounds of dried meat, 1,250 pounds of dried figs, as well as large quantities of beans, raisins, dried fish, wine, and brandy. The ship also carried church vestments for the priests, a big church bell and a variety of bargaining trinkets for the Indians.

Of the original company of soldiers, citizens and priests *(about 110)* only half actually arrived at San Diego. Desertion as well as death had depleted their numbers. The last of the four groups arrived in San Diego on July 1, 1769.

Although the Indians of this region were well-fed and more peaceful than the Indians of Baja California, some were suspicious of the newcomers, and protective barriers had to be built around the first Mission.

The original plans of the missionaries were to build and occupy the Missions, teach the Indians to be independent, and then, in ten years, leave. However, they were not able to follow this time schedule.

The moderate climate and abundant rains of California gave the new settlers much hope for their plans. Crops and animals prospered, and new Missions could be built on locations selected for their proximity to fields for crops and grazing, wood for fires, and fresh water.

From 1769 to 1824, the chain of Missions grew. The key Missions were those at San Diego, Monterey, and San Francisco. These three had natural harbors and were given presidios, or formal military installations. After these Missions were located, the others were spaced at intervals of about a day's travel on foot, mule, or horseback. As each settlement was planned, the priests, townspeople and the Indians who would be the Neophytes *(Catholic converts)*, and soldiers would settle in temporary housing of tules or wood and together would decide upon the best location for the Mission.

The earliest record of a Mexican-American woman in early California was of Doña Feliciana. She accompanied Father Crespi and the group of settlers in their "Mexico to Alta California" trip in 1775-76. She was a widow and, apparently, not only very intelligent, but talented as well. On the coldest nights, her singing brought cheer around the fire. She was gifted in getting along with others, and earned the highest respect of everyone.

The Spanish government supplied from $250 to $450 worth of materials yearly, and the Church's Pious Fund sent a starter sum of $1000 for each Mission's purchase of bells, church vestments, tools and seeds. Missions already established nearby would send animals for use and breeding stock, seeds and cuttings for planting, and any other items that could be helpful.

This is the floor plan of a finished Mission, generally made of adobe:

Adobe bricks were made of adobe clay, straw, sand, and water. Straw was often added to hold the mixture together. The mixture was put into wooden molds and sun-dried. These were laid together, end to end and side to side.

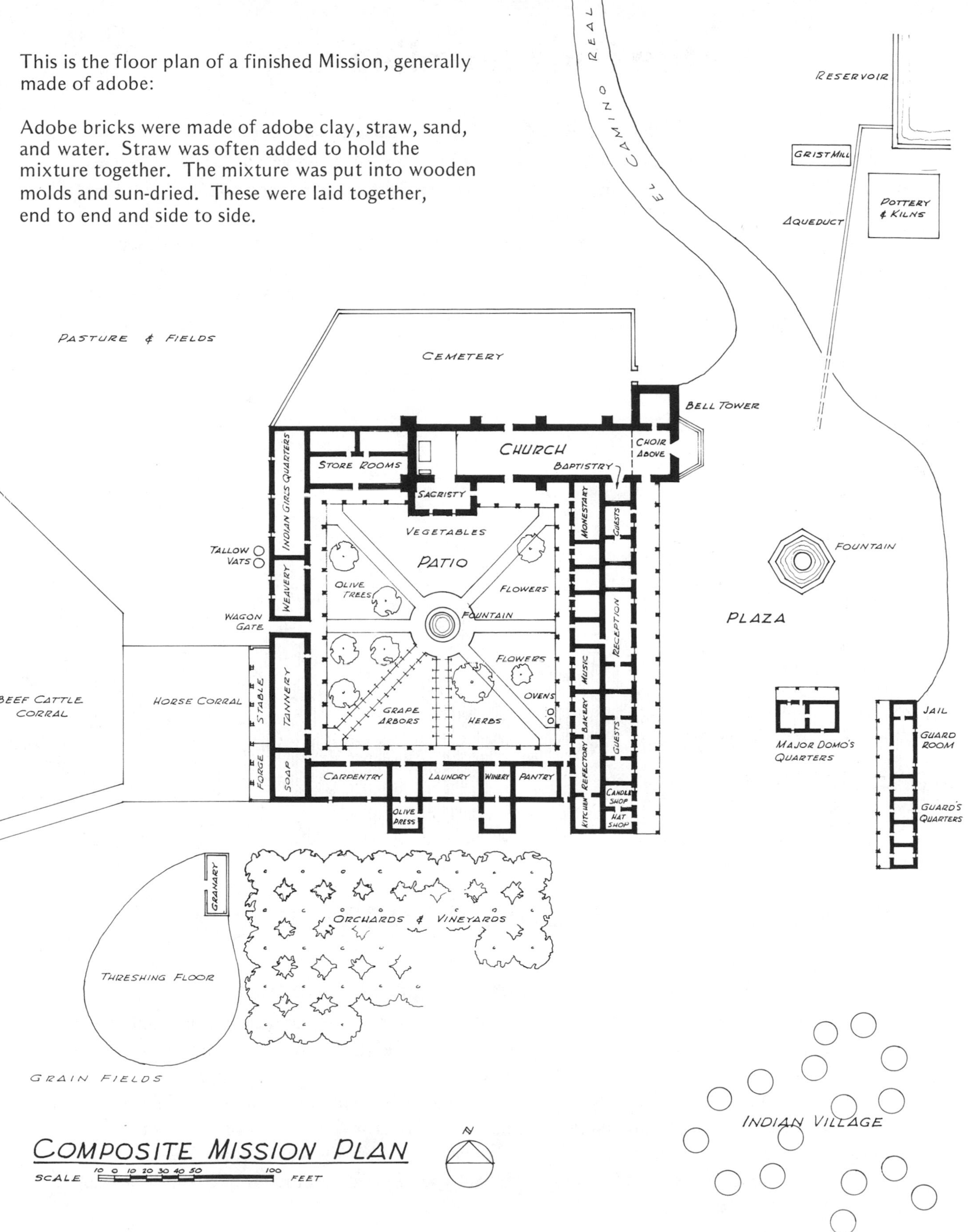

A Mile Long Traveling City

The First Settlers Walk to California

Mules, horses, burros, beef cattle, six tons of flour, cornmeal, sugar, chocolate and beans were among the supplies. Saddles and bridles, horseshoes and nails, tents and soldiers, and families, and cowboys, and priests completed the parade.

Babies were born, rivers were crossed, and Maria Feliciana Arballo sang in the desert snow. There was little food, and bad weather until Alta California was reached. Here the grass was green, fresh fish were plentiful, and clear water flowed in wonderful streams. On March 28, 1775 the settlers reached the Golden Gate and the site of the Presidio of San Francisco was dedicated.

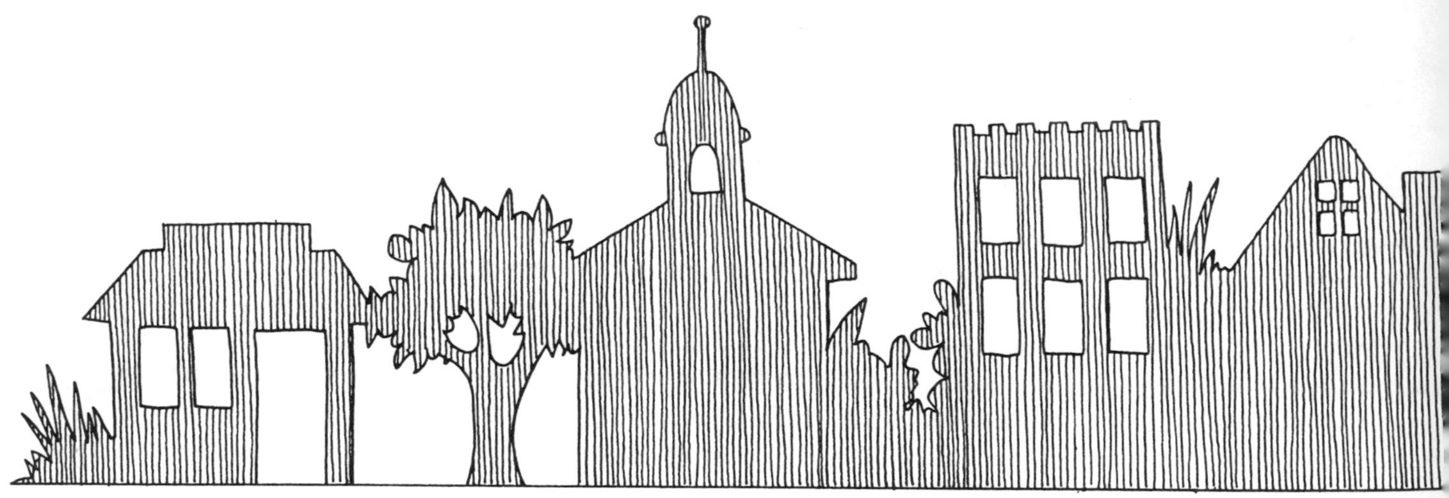

Una cuidad ambulante de una milla de largo

Los primeros pobladores caminan a California

Entre las provisiones llevaban mulas, caballos, burros, ganado para carne, seis toneladas de harina, harina de maía, azucar, chocolate y frijoles. Cerraban el desfile monturas, bridas, herraduras y clavos, tiendas de campaña y soldados, familias, vaqueros y curas.

Nacieron niños, cruzaron ríos, y María Feliciana Arballo cantó en las nieves del desierto. La comida escaseaba y hacia un tiempo inclemente hasta que llegaron a Alta California. Aquí había verdes prados, y peces en abundancia y el agua clara corría en hermosos riachuelos. El día 28 de marzo de 1775 los pobladores llegaron al Golden Gate y allí se dedicó el lugar que habría de ocupar el Presidio de San Francisco.

The Rancho Story

The Fathers who founded the Missions encouraged Mexicans and Spanish citizens with some soldiers to come and establish Ranchos and towns.

The Journal of One Rancher

My name is Pájaro. I own a rancho near the coast of Alta California; I am married and live with my wife and children on the edge of my land. I acquired it by measuring it with ropes held by my vaqueros. I then made a map of it and took the map to Monterey. (To be granted this land, I must be a Mexican citizen and a Catholic.) A government official will come back to the rancho with me. In the presence of him and the family from the neighboring rancho, I break branches off of trees, pull up grass, and scatter handfuls of earth. This makes the land legally mine.

El cuento de un rancho

Los padres que fundaron las misiones animaron a los ciudadanos mejicanos y españoles a que vinieran con algunos soldados a establecer ranchos y pueblos.

Diario de un ranchero

Me llamo Pájaro. Tengo un rancho cerca de la costa de Alta California. Estoy casado y vivo con mi esposa y mis hijos a la orilla de mis tierras. Las conseguí midiéndolas con cuerdas que sostenían mis vaqueros. Hice entonces un mapa de estas tierras y lo llevé a Monterrey. (Para que me den estas tierras debo ser mejicano y católico.) Vendrá conmigo al rancho un oficial del gobierno. Ante él y ante la familia del rancho contiguo, quiebro ramas de los árboles, arranco hierba y esparzo puñados de tierra. Esto da legalidad a mi propiedad de esta tierra.

Our home is well furnished. In our guest room, we have our finest silk pillow cases, silk sheets, and curtains. We also leave a bowl of money. The guests may take as much as they need, for it is never counted.

We live in the 1800s and our house is built on a square floor plan.

We have thirty Indian servants in all. Ten cook and serve, five do our sewing, six do our washing. Seven are vaqueros and the other two are personal servants.

My wife has much work to do. She supervises the servants who do the household work, but her main job is teaching our little girls to sew, make lace, embroider, and play instruments such as the guitar, violin, and flute.

Nuestro hogar está bien amueblado. En la habitación de los huéspedes tenemos nuestras mejores fundas de seda para las almohadas, sábanas de seda y cortinas. Tenemos también una escudilla llena de dinero. Los huéspedes pueden llevarse lo que necesiten pues jamás lo contamos.

Vivimos en los años de 1800 y nuestra casa está construida según un modelo de vivienda cuadrado.

Nos ayuda un total de treinta sirvientes indios. Diez guisan y sirven la comida, cinco se encargan de la costura, y seis lavan la ropa. Siete son vaqueros y los dos restantes son sirvientes personales.

Mi esposa tiene mucho trabajo. Se encarga de los sirvientes que hacen las tareas caseras, pero su trabajo fundamental es enseñarles a nuestras hijas a coser, hacer encaje, bordar y tocar instrumentos musicales como la guitarra, el violín y la flauta.

I do very different work, however. I am called el patrón. I tell my mayordomo (or foreman) what I want done. I also teach servants to plant trees and crops brought from Spain. We plant wheat, barley, corn, red beans, garbanzos, grapes, onions and garlic. Of trees, we plant olive, peach, apple, pears, and pomegranate. We grow these from cuttings that the Fathers at the Missions give us.

Rodeos

We have rodeos in the springtime, for that is when the calves are still following their mothers. Because of this, generally there is no dispute over which brand the calf will wear. The branding is done by a pair of men. One man will heat his iron in a small, hot fire made of brush while the other catches a calf. The calf is then tied and branded on the flank.

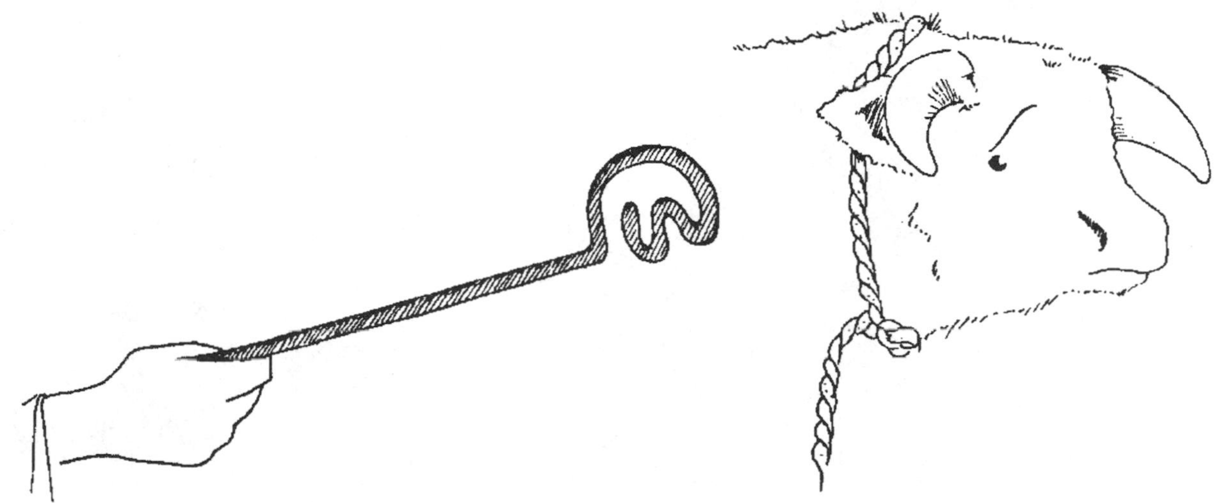

Yo, sin embargo, hago trabajo muy distinto. A mi me llaman el patrón. Yo le digo al mayordomo el trabajo que quiero que se haga. También les enseño a los sirvientes a plantar árboles y cosechas que se traen de España. Plantamos trigo, cebada, maíz, frijoles rojos, garbanzos, uvas, cebollas y ajos. Entre los árboles plantamos olivos, durazneros, manzanos, perales y granados. Estos los plantamos de los esquejes que nos dan los padres de las misiones.

Rodeos

Tenemos rodeos en la primavera porque en esta temporada los becerros aún siguen a sus mamás. Debido a esto generalmente no hay desacuerdo sobre la marca que llevará el becerro. Les ponen la marca un par de hombres. Uno de los hombres calienta el hierro sobre una hoguera de matorrales caliente y pequeña, mientras el otro atrapa al becerro. Amarran, entonces, al becerro y lo marcan en el costado.

We kill many cattle for their hides. Some of the Indians punch holes in the corners of the hides and set them out in the sun. After the hides are dry, we tan them. Putting a hide into the vat, we sprinkle ground oak bark on it, lay another hide on that one, treat it, etc. Then we soak them in water. Yankee ships come to trade with us, and buy our hides as they did with the Mission Fathers. We bring the hides to the seashore in carratas, a type of ox-drawn cart.

Loss of Rancho

I have decided to sell my rancho, for many of my friends are moving back home. I am selling it legally to a Yankee trader who bought and bartered for our hides. Our family will pack up and leave on May 16, 1842. I am reluctant to leave this rich land.

Matamos a mucho ganado para las pieles. Algunos de los indios hacen agujeros en las pieles y las estiran al sol para que se sequen. Cuando las pieles están secas, las curtimos. Colocamos la piel en una tina la espolvoreamos con corteza de roble molido, ponemos otra piel encima, la espolvoreamos, etc. Entonces las remojamos en agua. Los barcos yanquis comercian con nosotros y nos compran las pieles igual que se las compraban a los padres de las misiones. Traemos las pieles a la costa en carretas, una especie de carro tirado por bueyes.

Perdida del rancho

He decidido vender mi rancho porque muchos de mis amigos están volviendo a casa. Se lo voy a vender a un comerciante yanqui que nos compraba o cambiaba las pieles. Nuestra familia hará las maletas y se marchará el 16 de mayo de 1842. Siento mucho dejar esta rica tierra.

In an Acorn Shell

SECULARIZATION

After Mexico gained independence from Spain in 1810, financial support for the colonists dwindled and the Missions had to become self-supporting. The new Mexican government was not much interested in the Missions, and California's status as a Mexican colony was being threatened by the westward expansion of the United States.

Finally, in 1833, the secularization order was given. As originally planned by the Spanish system, the Missions were to be released and the churches themselves to go from the control of the missionary order to that of the parish priests. Other buildings were to become public property for the new *pueblo*, or town, and the land was turned over to the Native California families. Although this system had worked well in other Spanish colonies, it was a disaster in California; the Native Californians could not manage their new property and were easily deprived of their rights by land speculators. The buildings were sold or simply occupied, and property often allowed to deteriorate and disappear. The Missions themselves were nearly forgotten as the entire system was destroyed.

Secularization failed, it would appear, partly because of everyone's land greed. With priests, Indians, and other Mission participants gone, the church lands were frequently taken by the first persons on the spot.

WHAT THE MISSIONS OVERCAME – HARD TIMES CHART

Mission	*Earthquake*	*Raids by Native Californians*	*Bouchard The Pirate*	*Native Californian Epidemics*	*Secularization*	*Sold*	*Returned to Church*
San Diego de Alcalá	1803	1775			1834	1846	1862
San Carlos Borromeo de Carmelo			1818		1834		
San Antonio de Padua							1862
San Gabriel Arcángel	1812	1834				1846	1859
San Luís Obispo de Tolosa	1830	1776	1818		1835	1845	1859
San Juan de Capistrano	1812		1818	1801		1845	
San Francisco de Asís				1838	1834		1857
Santa Clara de Asís	1812,1818			Plague Mice	1836		
San Buenaventura	1812		1818		1836	1846	1862
Santa Bárbara	1800,1812	1824			1834	1846	1865
La Purísima Concepción	1812	1824		1844	1834	1845	
Santa Cruz	1857		1818		1834		
Nuestra Señora de La Soledad				1802	1835	1846	1859
San José		1817,1826, 1829			1834	1846	1865
San Juan Bautista					1835		
San Miguel Arcángel						1846	1859
San Fernando Rey de España	1812				1834		1861
San Luís Rey de Francia					1834	1846	1865
Santa Inés	1812	1824			1834	1846	1862
San Rafael Arcángel		1832			1834	1846	1855
San Francisco Solano		1826			1834	1880	

WHAT HAPPENED TO THE INDIANS?

Here are some answers, you readers, keep looking for more.

1. **Disease: the largest killer**
   The Indians had no natural immunity to such epidemics as malaria, small pox, and measles.

2. **There was almost no medical help for anyone in the Missions**

3. **Culture shock:**
   The Indians were forced to adapt to Mission life and it was a very different life than had been theirs. Of necessity, the Missions were agriculturally self-sufficient, long hours were put in, with few mintues for rest.

The first generation Mission Indians had had great variety in their lives in their tribes and villages. These early Indians felt a loss of freedom and self-expression at the Missions.

Apparently few children were born to Mission Indian couples, possibly because of the strain of adjusting to a completely new way of life. According to Heizer and Elsasser, infant mortality was very high.

At the end of the Mission period, from 1769 to 1834, it has been reported that there were one half as many Indians in this Mission area as there had been in the beginning.

After Mexican Independence in 1834, came the Rancho period. During this time the Indians were generally used as slaves or peons. They cleaned the houses and farmed the land and worked the cattle of their wealthy patrons.

The Indians living away from the Mission areas were pretty much left alone.

Though the Gold Rush didn't take place in Mission locations, its effect on other Indian tribes was significant. Miners and settlers swarmed into the interior valley and the gold bearing regions of the Sierra. The Indians native to those areas had known of the abundance of gold, but not until the white man came to claim it did the gold cause trouble. The miners poured in, and there was competition for food; many massacres of the Indians ensued.

By 1910, the Indian population of California fell to about 20,000 people.

We see in this Mission story, one culture imposing itself upon another. The Spanish appeared to feel that they could give the Indians a better life through the Mission system. Did they?

Were the Indians safer in adobe brick buildings in earthquakes; healthier around the white man's diseases? Were they more contented eating the white man's food? Did it comfort them to serve a god who was strange to them?

Where have all the Indians gone? With the children around you explore these questions and think of many more. If we cannot grow from the examination of those who lived before us, then they have almost lived in vain.

THE ROLE OF WOMEN

Women were of vital importance in the history of early California. We have a great deal to learn of them and from the time. However, the role of women in California's early history cannot be fully dealt with here. The records of many women who were active in public life, at present, have not been discovered. The work of historians continues. Previously lost treasures of documents are being found every year.

Our state is rich in the resources of a multi-ethnic society. We now have many Mexican-Americans, Indians and Blacks among our members of the California population. We appreciate their contributions to the total citizenry, but encourage always the texture of diversity among all members of our society.

HANDICAPPED CHILDREN

There are no clear records of the place of children with handicaps in early California.

The emphasis is placed here on giving equal rights for everyone, no matter what age, sex or ethnic background, or physical or mental endowments they might have possessed.

REJUVENATION

During the years, an occasional photographer or painter would share a visual fascination for the Missions through pictures taken, drawn or painted. Some of these pictures grace the walls of special Missions today.

Through the early 20th century, as the automobile took us more places and as El Camino Real developed, Mission restoration began. Sir Henry Downie, Curator of the Carmel Mission, known as the Mission restoration architect, used time and money to generate much enthusiasm for this exciting project.

At this writing all of the Missions have gone through, or are going through restoration and are living again.

Most Missions are living, perhaps most vitally as parish churches. Two are California State Parks. In this restored, "live again" life, tourism is stimulated, weddings are celebrated, funerals are conducted, and baptisms performed.

Mission authenticity is looked for and respected!

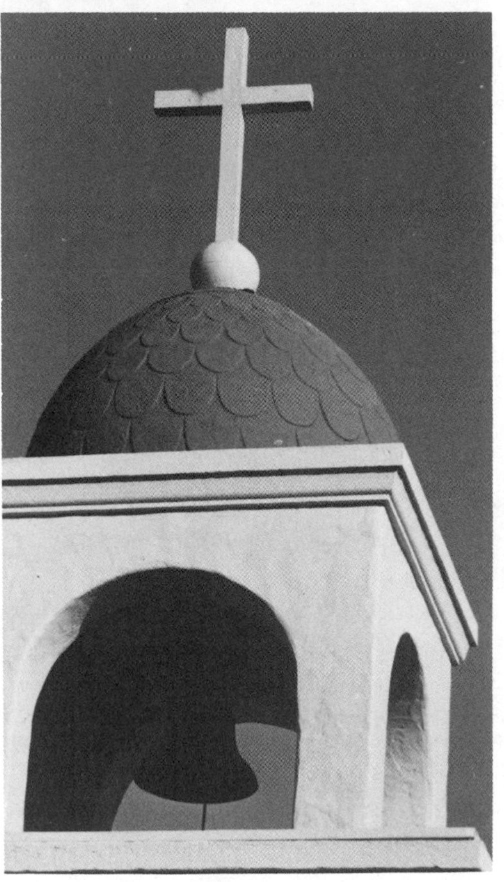

A LIVING MISSION

The Palo Mission – address to Mission San Luís.

First founding: 1816. An asistencia or helping Mission, Palo is also an inland Mission. In 1818, the chapel of San Antonio was enlarged and completed. Two large granaries were built, as were dormitories for boys and men and for girls and women. These were fanhioned from adobe and had red tile roofs.

Palo Mission Native Californians are Shoshoneans, called Luisenis since early Mission days. The Mission was abandoned with the others, but in May 1902 it was bought by the Landmark Society.

In 1956, a complete reconstruction was promised which was to include the founding of a school. There were problems and roadblocks, but today Palo Mission is restored and has a successful school, and a church membership of Native Americans which is unique in the present California Mission System. Palo Mission is alive, well, and an example of "living again."

ADDRESSES OF MISSIONS TODAY

Mission Basilica
San Diego de Alcalá
10818 San Diego Mission Rd.
San Diego, CA 92108

Mission San Carlos
Borromeo Basilica
P.O. Box 2235
Carmel, CA 93921

San Antonio de Padua Mission
P.O. Box 803
Jolon, CA 93928

Mission San Gabriel
537 West Mission Dr.
San Gabriel, CA 91776

Mission San Luis Obispo
941 Chorro St.
San Luis Obispo, CA 93402

Mission Dolores
3321 16th St.
San Francisco, CA 94114

Mission San Juan Capistrano
P.O. Box 697
San Juan Capistrano, CA 92693

Mission San José
P. O. Box 3276
San Jose, CA 94538

Mission San Buenaventura
211 East Main St.
Ventura, CA 93001

Old Mission
2201 Laguna St.
Santa Barbara, CA 93105

Area Manager
Mission La Purisima Concepción
RFD #102
Lompoc, CA 93436

Mission Santa Cruz
126 High St.
Santa Cruz, CA 95060

Old Mission
c/o Our Lady of Soledad Parish
P.O. Box 506
Soledad, CA 93960

Mission Santa Clara
Santa Clara University
500 El Camino Real (Box 3217)
Santa Clara, CA 95053-3217

Mission San Juan Bautista
P.O. Box 41
San Juan Bautista, CA 95045

Old Mission
San Miguel, CA 93451

San Fernando Rey de Espana
15151 Mission Blvd.
San Fernando, CA 91345

Mission San Luís Rey
4050 Mission Blvd.
San Luis Rey, CA 92068

Mission Santa Inés
1750 Mission Dr.
Solvang, CA 93463

Mission San Rafael Arcángel
1104 - 5th St.
San Rafael, CA 94901

Area Manager
Mission San Francisco Solano
P.O. Box 167
Sonoma, CA 95476

Visualizing Historical Events

FLANNEL BOARDS

Cover a board or large sheet of cardboard with felt, flannel, or sandpaper. Cut out pictures from paper or magazines, for Mission days story telling. Glue felt, sandpaper or flannel on the back of the pictures. Use these for storytelling by putting them on and off and here and there.

Materials — Scissors
— Paper
— Magazine pictures
— Colored paper
— Big board - felt, flannel or sandpaper
— Glue

MISSION FROM BAKER'S CLAY

Mix; add color; and wrap to insure moistness. You can roll the walls and add texture, as shown. Put these little missions together by wedging or pressing corners together. Bake at 325° for 2 hours. You may save some assembly work until the end.

Materials – Salt, flour, water
– Tempera paint
– Plastic wrap
– Model materials

DIORAMAS

Make a real scene depicting Indian, Mission or rancho days in 3-D. Put paper tabs on paper figures to make them stand. Sponges make good bushes and bushy trees. Paint them with tempera.

Materials

— Shoe boxes	— Colored paper
— Scissors	— Sponges - twigs - etc.
— Paste or glue	— Magazine pictures

NEWSPAPER

Make a newspaper; use various parts of the paper to shed light on the life of a particular event, such as earthquake news, recipes, the latest fashions, and growing things.

How to Do It

Really study the newspaper and its various parts. Determine who will do what, such as feature writer, travel, economics, or bartering. You may want to bill jobs, such as editor-in-chief, news editor, weather forecaster, etc. Advertise for adobe makers, muleteers, and gardeners.

Application

This will give participants a chance to really look over various mission times and rewrite special events and daily life that took place during this time.

Materials — Will depend on your way with the newspaper

BULLETIN BOARDS

Select your theme and use both written and pictured concepts to bring it to life. Notice the border of Mission designs.

Materials — Display materials
— Scissors
— Glue
— Colored paper for background
— Push pins

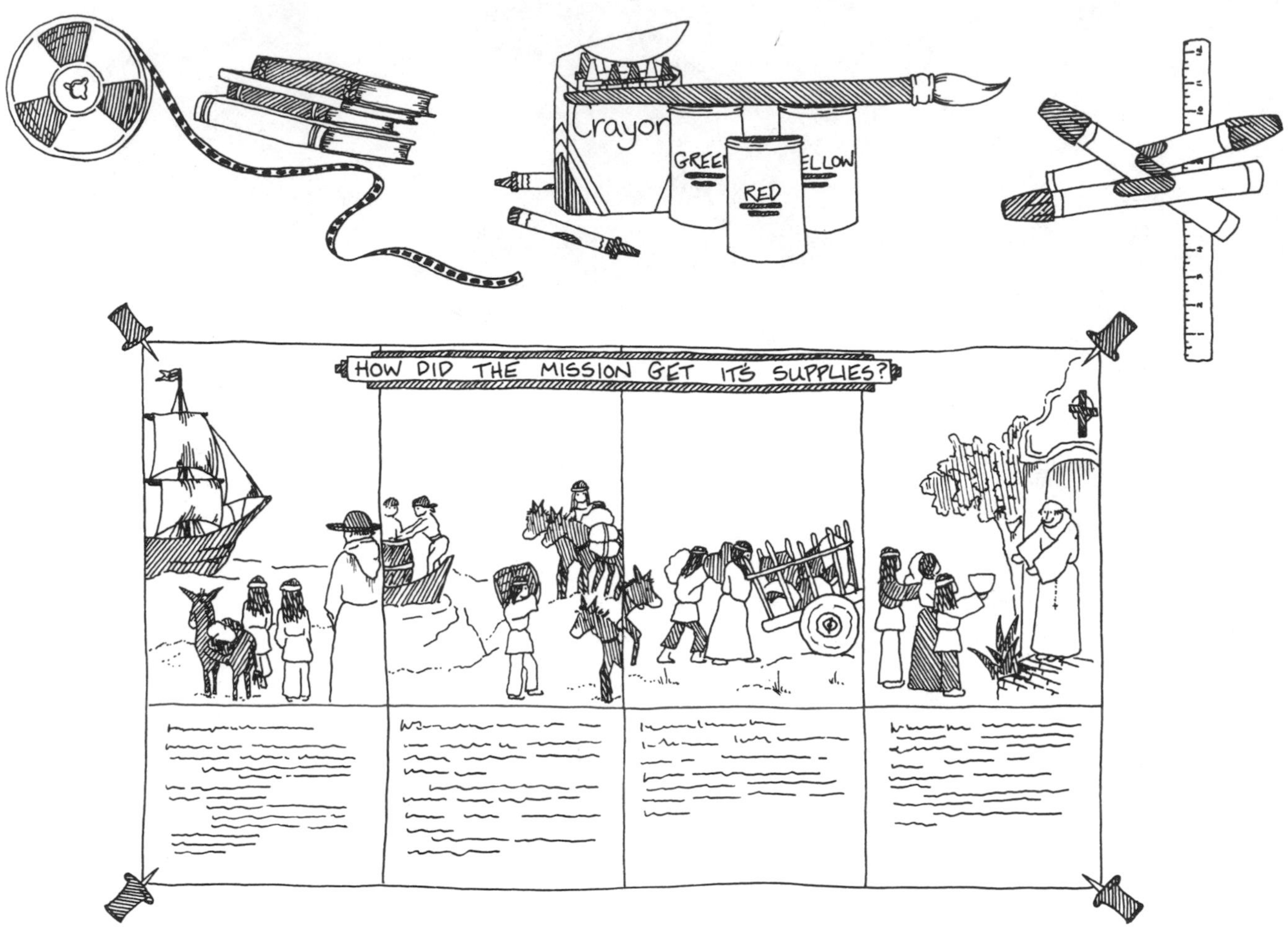

STORY BOARDS

Background: traditionally, motion pictures are started with storyboards – a sequence of pictures and the accompanying script, as shown.

Be sure to explore the topic, such as Mission supplies, so the artist-writer can approach the task with confidence. Paints, crayons, and felt pens are the best tools. Any phase of California history is suitable for storyboards.

Materials – Paper, pencils or pens
– Crayons, paint or felt pen markers

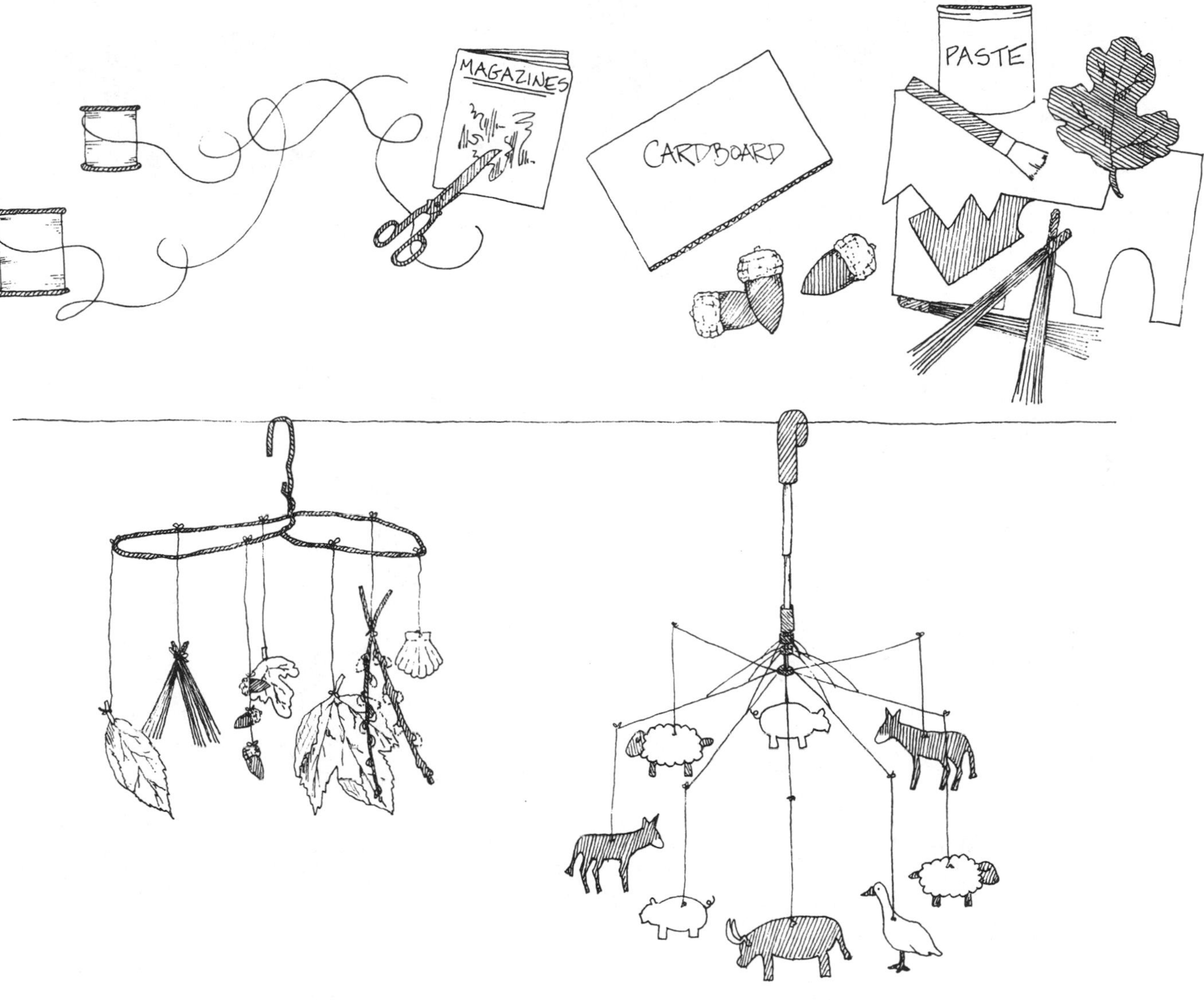

MISSION MOBILES

Natural materials found in California or Mission themes, such as animals cut from cardboard and painted are fine. Magazine pictures may be glued onto cardboard and cut, too. Notice the coat hanger and umbrella mobiles?

Materials – Wire hangers or umbrella
- Magazine pictures mounted on cardboard
- Nature materials
- Thread
- Scissors

MURALS

1. Select a theme
2. Select a group or do the mural yourselves.
3. List contents of the mural. Let it make a statement or tell a story.
4. Sketch it on butcher, shelf or manila paper in white chalk.

Use paint, chalk *(use dry chalk, wet chalk, wet and sugared chalk, or chalk dipped in canned milk),* crayons, cut paper or magazine pictures for telling the story. These can be telling a single event or a series, as shown.

Materials — Paper
— Chalk
— Crayons
— Magazine
— Colored paper
— Scissors
— Glue

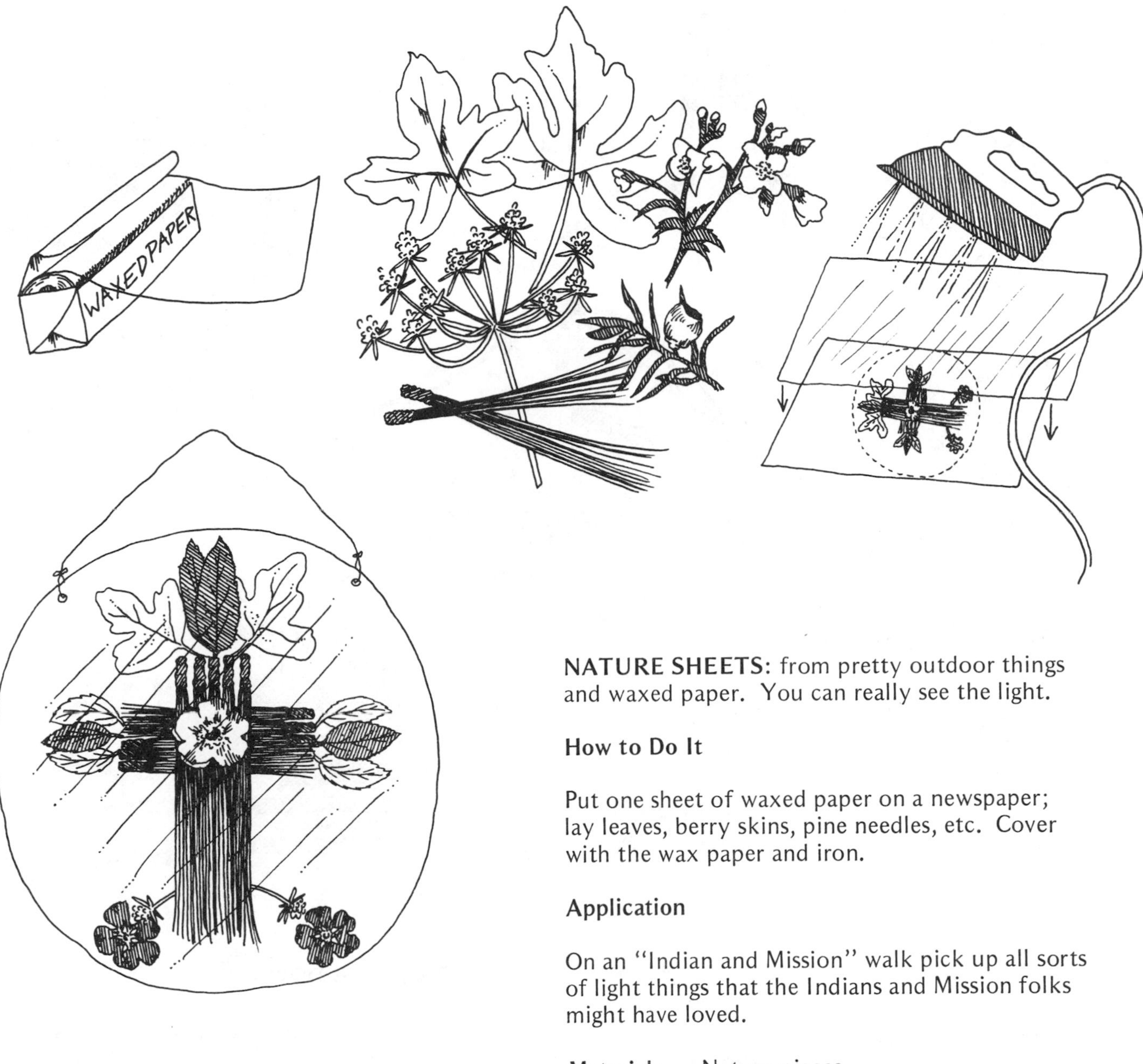

NATURE SHEETS: from pretty outdoor things and waxed paper. You can really see the light.

How to Do It

Put one sheet of waxed paper on a newspaper; lay leaves, berry skins, pine needles, etc. Cover with the wax paper and iron.

Application

On an "Indian and Mission" walk pick up all sorts of light things that the Indians and Mission folks might have loved.

Materials — Nature pieces
— Waxed paper
— Iron

A CALIFORNIA RUB DOWN

Using white, manila or typing paper with crayons rubbed over such surfaces as those shown. If these are nicely cut and matted they will make good looking wall pieces.

Materials – Paper
– Crayons
– Textured surface

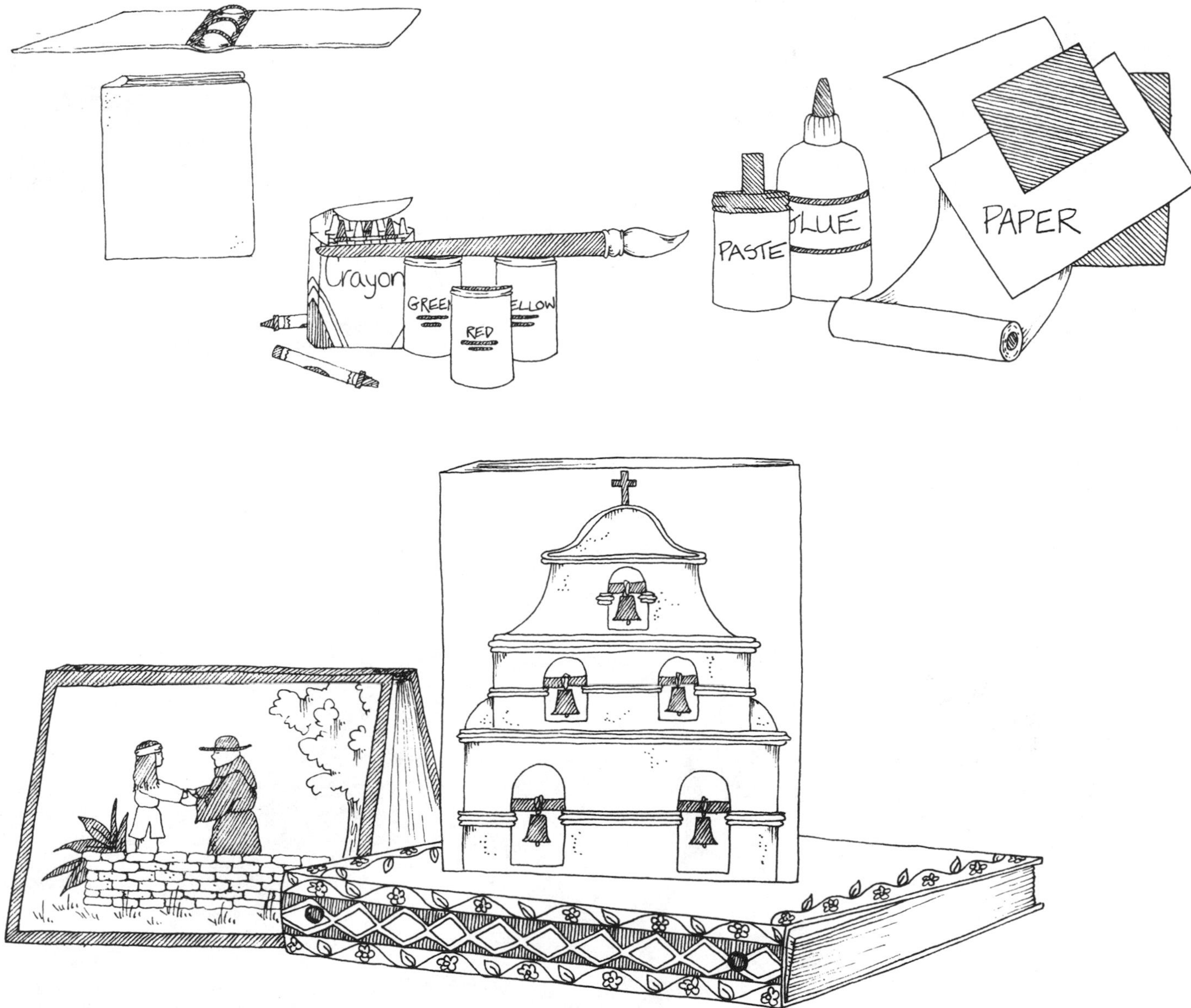

NOTEBOOK COVERS

Use a binder or make a paper or cardboard folder for holding Mission papers and pictures. Center on a theme and decorate for open house at school or happy saving at home. Crayons, paints or cut paper are fine for decorating.

Materials — Notebooks
— Colored paper
— Paint
— Crayons
— Paste
— Scissors

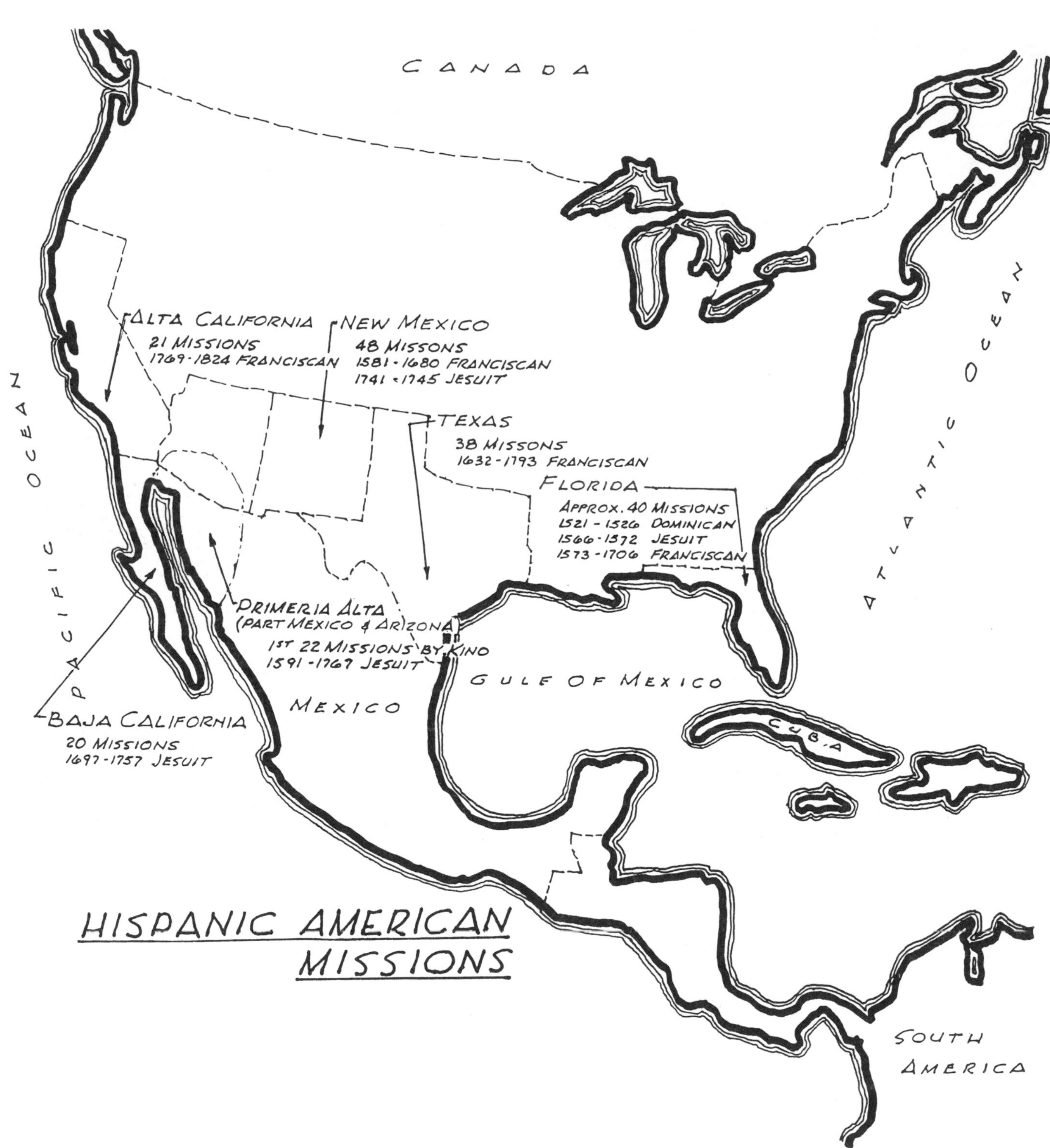
CANADA
ALTA CALIFORNIA
21 MISSIONS
1769-1824 FRANCISCAN
NEW MEXICO
48 MISSONS
1581-1680 FRANCISCAN
1741-1745 JESUIT
TEXAS
38 MISSONS
1632-1793 FRANCISCAN
FLORIDA
APPROX. 40 MISSIONS
1521-1526 DOMINICAN
1566-1572 JESUIT
1573-1706 FRANCISCAN
PRIMERIA ALTA
(PART MEXICO & ARIZONA)
1ST 22 MISSIONS BY KINO
1591-1767 JESUIT
GULF OF MEXICO
MEXICO
BAJA CALIFORNIA
20 MISSIONS
1697-1757 JESUIT
PACIFIC OCEAN
ATLANTIC OCEAN
CUBA
SOUTH AMERICA
HISPANIC AMERICAN MISSIONS

Mission San Francisco de la Espada
San Antonio, Texas

Mission San José de Laguna
Laguna Pueblo, New Mexico

George Kusko
1994
Mission San José de Tumacácori
Tubac, Arizona

Mission Stories
Historias de Las Misiones

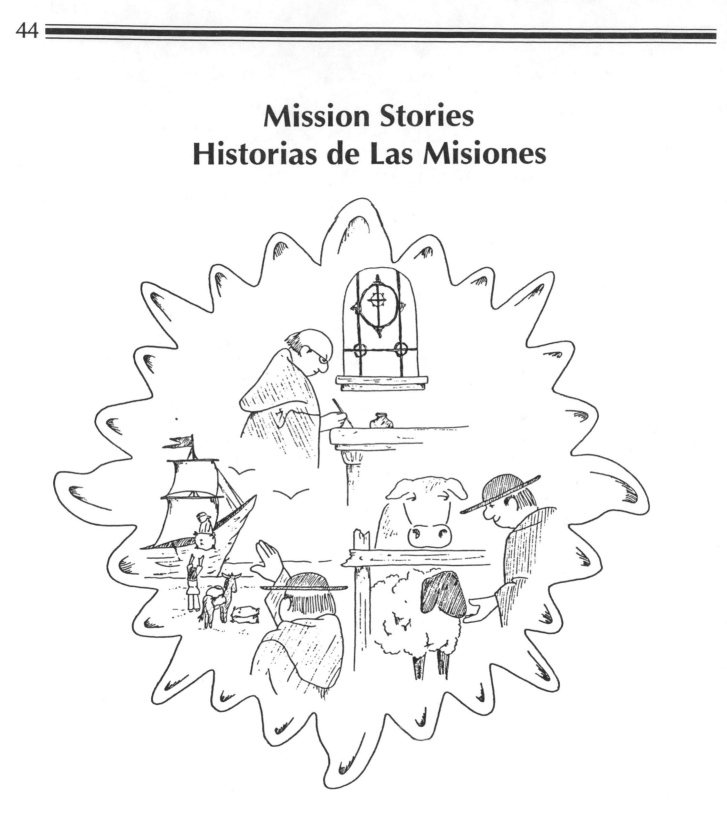

Day In The Life of A Padre
Un dia en La Vida de un Padre

Write a Mission Report

Outline

I. Founding
 A. Father Serra
 B. Father Lasuen
 C. Indians

II. The First buildings
 A. Materials used
 B. Plan for the buildings

III. Early years at the Mission
 A. The big fire
 B. Rebuilding of the church

IV. The Indians
 A. What tribes
 B. Their houses, jobs and skills

V. The mission irrigation
 A. Fountains
 B. Ditches

VI. Jobs for the Padres at the mission
 A. Livestock
 B. Crops
 C. Education of Indians
 D. Record keeping

Founding Missions

Hello and Good-bye to Silver and Pearls

In 1697 the King of Spain had heard that Baja California had mountains of silver and lakes of pearls. (map) He wanted the silver, he wanted the pearls and he wanted the natives of Baja. Priests were set to build a chain of Missions. The Native Californians were to live at the missions, to become Catholics and Spanish speaking citizens of Spain. 20 missions were built. They were a 70 year failure. The land was rocky, the weather was hot; Crops didn't grow. Thousands of Native Americans got sick and died from the "White Man's Sicknesses."

Las Misiones

Saludo y adiós a la plata y las perlas

En 1697 el rey de España había oído que Baja California tenía montañas de plata y lagos de perlas. (mapa) Quería la plata, quería las perlas y quería los indígenas de Baja. Enviaron a los curas a construir una cadena de misiones. Los indígenas de California vivirían en las misiones, se harían católicos, hablarían español y serían súbditos de España. Construyeron 20 misiones. Fueron un fracaso de 70 años. La tierra era rocosa, el clima caliente. No crecían las cosechas. Miles de indígenas enfermaron y murieron de "La enfermedad del hombre blanco."

San Diego de Alcalá

The First Mission in Alta California

July 16, 1769 Father Serra blessed and placed a cross on the ground to mark the start of this mission. The Spanish settlers had walked or sailed from Mexico. More than half died on the trip. The Native Americans stayed away at first.

On a night in November 1775, an army of hundreds of Native Californians attacked, burned the mission and killed Father Jayme.

The fathers rebuilt the mission, planted crops and raised livestock. Soon Native Americans joined and the mission was a success.

La primera misión en Alta California

El 16 de julio de 1769 el Padre Serra bendijo y puso una cruz en el suelo para marcar el comienzo de esta misión. Los pobladores españoles habían llegado caminando o navegando desde México. Más de la mitad murieron durante el viaje. Los indígenas americanos se mantuvieron alejados al principio.

Una noche do noviembre de 1775, un ejército de cientos de indígenas californianos atacaron la misión y mataron al Padre Jayme.

Los padres volvieron a construir la misión, se dedicaron a la labranza y a la cría de ganado. Pronto los indígenas americanos se les unieron y la misión se hizo un éxito.

San Carlos Borromeo de Carmelo

A Fishy Surprise

In 1602 the Spanish Explorer Viscaino wrote about Monterey Bay and the beautiful oak grove nearby.

168 years later, Portola used Viscaino's journal, thought he found the same oaks and built a cross to mark the spot.

One year later, it is told, Father Serra and his group of mission builders and presidio settlers found the cross. It had been decorated by the Native Americans with arrows, meat, feathers, shell fish and a string of sardines.

Father Serra blest the spot, the mission was built nearby and it became the headquarters of all of the California Missions.

A Fishy Surprise
Una sorpresa en la cruz

Una sorpresa en la cruz

En 1602, el explorador español Viscaino escribió sobre la Bahía de Monterrey y sobre el robledo situado cerca de allí.

168 años más tarde, Portola usó el diario de Viscaino, pensó que había encontrado los mismos robles y construyó una cruz para marcar el lugar.

Se cuenta que un año más tarde, el Padre Serra y su grupo de fundadores de misiones y pobladores de presidios encontraron la cruz. La habían decorado los indígenas americanos con flechas, carne, plumas, mariscos y una cuerda de sardinas.

El Padre Serra bendijo el lugar y la misión que construyeron cerca de allí se convirtió en la sede principal de todas las misiones de California.

San Antonio de Padua

The Mission and the Army

Father Serra founded this mission in a pretty valley south of Carmel. It was the first not to be built on the coast and is in a grove of oak trees. The friendly Native Americans were slow in joining and giving up their religions.

Over time as the mission grew, a very complex water system and flour mill were developed. These brought fame to the mission and water to farmers years later.

The army bought land and built Camp Hunter Ligget in the 1940s. It is just down the road. If the soldiers and the buildings weren't there, a trip to the mission would take you back in time to 1772.

The Mission and the Army
La misión y el ejército

La misión y el ejército

El Padre Serra fundó esta misión en un bonito valle al sur de Carmel. Fue la primera misión que no se construyó en la costa y se encuentra situada en un robledo. Los amigables indígenas tardaron en unirse a la misión y en abandonar sus propias religiones.

Con el tiempo, según fue creciendo la misión, se fue desarrollando un complejo sistema de agua y un molino de harina. Esto le trajo fama a la misión y agua a los agricultores años después.

El ejército compró tierra y construyó el campamento Hunter Ligget en los años cuarenta. Se encuentra cerca de allí, camino abajo. Si no estuvieran allí los soldados y los edificios, un viaje a la misión sería un viaje al pasado, al año 1772.

San Gabriel Arcángel

The Mission at the Crossroads

This mission was such a success it was called, "Mother of California Farming." The lands had good soil, a gentle climate and plenty of water. The fathers worked hard and the Native Americans were friendly. The church owned so much land it is hard to imagine the acres of crops and numbers of animals that were raised.

As time passed three land routes came together and formed the crossroads at the mission. These were routes from Mexico, from the east and the north. These brought people and businesses to Los Angeles. San Gabriel lost its farm feeling and is now right in the middle of a big city.

The Mission at the Crossroads
La misión en el cruce de caminos

La misión en el cruce de caminos

Esta misión tuvo tanto éxito que la llamaron "la madre de la agricultura de California." La tierra era fértil, el clima templado y había agua en abundancia. Los padres trabajaban mucho y los indígenas americanos eran amigables. La iglesia tenía tanta tierra que resulta difícil imaginar la cantidad de acres labrados y el número de animales que se criaban.

Con el paso del tiempo, llegaron a cruzarse tres caminos en la misión. Eran las rutas de México, del este y del norte. Estos caminos traían gente y mercancías a Los Angeles. San Gabriel perdió su ambiente agrícola y se encuentra hoy día en el centro de una gran ciudad.

San Luis Obispo

The Bear Facts

The signs say, "Watch out for the grizzly bears." In the year 1772 it was the bears who needed help.

Mission San Luis Obispo is in a lovely spot named the valley of the bears. As the story goes, while this mission was being built, everyone was starving for food.

They ate the grizzly bears. Once they killed 9,000 pound of bear meat and had a real feast. The Native Americans later gave them seeds to plant in exchange for bear meat. Soon the mission gardens were full of beans, corn and other crops and the bears again could roam the hills without fear of becoming somebody's dinner.

The Bear Facts
Es una cuestión de osos

Es una cuestión de osos

El cartel dice, "Cuidado con los osos." En el año 1772 eran los osos los que necesitaban ayuda.

La Misión San Luis Obispo es un lugar encantador que lleva el nombre el valle de los osos. Según cuentan, mientras construían esta misión, todos pasaron mucha hambre.

Se comieron los osos grises. En una ocasión mataron 9.000 libras de carne de oso y celebraron una gran fiesta. Más tarde los indígenas les dieron semillas para plantar a cambio de carne de oso. En poco tiempo los huertos de la misión se llenaron de frijoles, maíz y otras hortalizas y los osos pudieron una vez más recorrer los montes sin temor de convertirse en alimento para la mesa.

San Francisco de Asís

The Mission by the Narrow Gate

The great San Francisco bay was slow to be discovered because the entrance to the bay was so narrow. Portola saw what a great bay it was on his second trip north. Orders were given to found missions, a presidio and town at once.

Juan Bautista de Anza led 240 settlers and 1,000 farm animals from Sonora Mexico to San Francisco. They crossed rivers, deserts and mountains. They arrived with four more people, babies born on the trip.

The mission had a struggle, crops did poorly, and Native Americans died from disease or ran away. The church, however, built in 1791 still stands and is beautiful!

The Mission by the Narrow Gate
La misión al lado del pasaje estrecho

La misión al lado del pasaje estrecho

Tardaron en descubrir la gran bahía de San Francisco porque la entrada a la bahía era tan estrecha. Portola se dio cuenta de la grandeza de la bahía durante su segundo viaje al norte. Se ordenó la inmediata construcción de una misión, un presidio y un pueblo.

Juan Bautista de Anza se encargó de llevar a 240 pobladores y 1.000 animales domésticos de Sonora, México a San Francisco. Cruzaron ríos, desiertos y montañas. Llegaron con cuatro personas adicionales, niños que habían nacido durante el viaje.

Fueron tiempos difíciles para la misión. Las cosechas eran pobres y los indígenas morían de enfermedades o huían. ¡La iglesia, sin embargo, construida en 1791 sigue en pie y es hermosa!

San Juan de Capistrano

The Mission for the Birds - - -

This Mission was founded on October 30, 1775. It was a success right away. The Native Americans were friendly, the climate mild. It is near the ocean, has a breeze and rich soil.

Who knows when for sure, but for as long as people remember a huge flock of swallows has come to San Juan de Capistrano on their migration south sometime in October, and North in March. It is a wonderful sight and the exact date may depend on the weather.

Forty Native Americans were killed in the 1812 earthquake and the church was never rebuilt, but it hasn't kept the birds away.

The Mission for the Birds - - -
La misión para los pájaros

La misión para los pájaros

Se fundó esta misión el 30 de octubre de 1775. Fue un éxito inmediato. Los indígenas americanos eran amistosos, el clima cálido. Está cerca del mar, tiene brisas y suelo fértil.

No hay quién lo sepa por cierto, pero desde tiempos remotos una enorme bandada de golondrinas viene a San Juan de Capistrano en su viaje migratorio al sur en octubre y al norte en marzo. Es un espectáculo maravilloso y la fecha exacta puede que dependa del tiempo que haga.

Murieron cuarenta indígenas americanos en el terremoto de 1812 y no se ha vuelto a reconstruir la iglesia, pero esto no ha evitado que vuelvan los pájaros.

Santa Clara de Asis

The Mission With the College Education

English and Russian settlers were interested in controlling the San Francisco Bay. Mission Santa Clara was built to help protect the bay area for Spain.

Floods, earthquake and fires destroyed the mission and it was rebuilt seven times. It became successful and was second in wealth only to San Gabriel.

In 1851 when California was a state the mission was turned over to English speaking priests, the Jesuits.

In 1855 it became Santa Clara College and later the University of Santa Clara.

The Mission With the College Education
La misión con una educación universitaria

La misión con una educación universitaria

A los pobladores ingleses y rusos les interesaba controlar la bahía de San Francisco. La misión Santa Clara se construyó para proteger la bahía para España.

Inundaciones, terremotos incendios destruyeron la misión que tuvieron que volver a construir siete veces. La misión fue por fin un éxito y solamente San Gabriel la superaba en riqueza.

En 1851 cuando California ya era un estado tomaron control de la misión los Jesuitas, unos curas de habla inglesa.

En 1855 se convirtió en el Santa Clara College y más tarde en la Universidad de Santa Clara.

San Buenaventura

The Mission That Waited 12 Years!

Mission San Buenaventura was to be the third in the mission chain. When San Francisco Bay was discovered, Father Serra changed his plans and this became the ninth.

The mission prospered. Many kinds of fruit and tropical plants were among the crops. A water system seven miles long was built to water the grain fields.

Native Americans there were the Chumash. They were a very advanced California tribe. They built boats, were good seamen and fishermen. The women were weavers who made their baskets watertight.

The city of Ventura has grown around the church but a new plaza in front has added a sense of space and history.

The Mission That Waited 12 Years!
¡La misión que esperó 12 años!

La misión que esperó 12 años!

La misión San Buenaventura debería haber sido la tercera misión. Cuando descubrieron la bahía de San Francisco, el Padre Serra cambió de parecer y San Buenaventura se convirtió en la novena.

La misión prosperó. En los huertos se encontraban muchas clases de fruta y plantas tropicales. Para regar los campos de cereales construyeron un sistema de riego de siete millas de extensión.

Los Chumash eran los indígenas de esta región. Era una tribu californiana muy avanzada. Construían barcos y eran buenos navegantes y pescadores. Las mujeres eran hilanderas y construían cestas impermeables. La ciudad de Ventura ha ido creciendo alrededor de la iglesia pero la construcción de una nueva plaza delante de la iglesia ha añ adido una sensación de espacio e historia.

Santa Bárbara

The Queen of the Missions

The explorer Viscaino discovered and named Santa Bárbara in about 1602. The Presidio, the city and the mission all have that name.

In 1780 the Presidio was built and the army moved in so the area would be protected Six years later, in 1786, the Franciscans founded the mission. They have been there ever since..

The Native Americans were the Chumash, a very advanced group. With the Franciscans they farmed, painted, played music, built a fine water system and ran a hospital.

This is a real jewel in the mission chain or necklace.

The Queen of the Missions
La reina de las misiones

La reina de las misiones

El explorador Viscaino descubrió y nombró Santa Bárbara alrededor de 1602. El presidio, la ciudad y la misión todos llevan ese nombre.

En 1780 se construyó el presidio y el ejército se trasladó allí para proteger esta zona. Seis años después, en 1786, los franciscanos fundaron la misión. Llevan allí desde entonces.

Los indígenas americanos en esta zona eran los Chumash, un grupo muy avanzado. Con los franciscanos labraban la tierra, pintaban, tocaban música, construyeron un buen sistema de agua y llevaban un hospital.

Está es una verdadera joya en la cadena o collar de misiones.

La Purisima Concepción

The Bad Luck, Good Luck Mission

This mission was built in a lovely place. Crops and livestock grew. Many Native Americans joined.

25 years later it was destroyed by an earthquake, the dam broke and flooded the ruins.

There was no rain for several years and crops didn't grow. There was so little food the Native Americans were angry and destroyed much of the mission.

Almost 90 years later the mission was given to the United States as a present. Enough men were sent, time and money were given to rebuild the mission. The good luck is still with it and it is open to visitors. Go and see for yourself.

The Bad Luck, Good Luck Mission
La misión de la mala y la buena suerte

La misión de la mala y la buena suerte

Construyeron esta misión en un lugar precioso. Crecieron el ganado y las cosechas. Se unieron a la misión muchos indígenas americanos.

25 años más tarde un terremoto destruyó la misión, se rompió la presa y se inundaron las ruinas.

Pasaron varios años sin lluvia y las cosechas no crecían. Había tan poca comida que los indígenas americanos se enojaron y destruyeron gran parte de la misión.

Unos 90 años más tarde regalaron la misión a los Estados Unidos. Dedicaron suficientes hombres, tiempo y dinero para reconstruir la misión. Sigue la buena fortuna y la misión permanece abierta. Ve y la verás.

Santa Cruz

One Thing and Then Another

Where the river meets the bay with deer, rabbits, pine trees and berries, the Santa Cruz Mission was founded in 1791.

The governor started the town of Branciforte in 1796, across the river from the mission. It was filled with trouble makers from Mexico who came there instead of going to jail.

They caused terrible problems at the mission. Later, rain and wind almost destroyed the building.

Father Quintana was murdered in his bed at the mission. The mission was secularized in 1834 and then two earthquakes destroyed the remains. A smaller church was built in 1931 and is still there.

One Thing and Then Another
Una cosa tras otra

Una cosa tras otra

En el sitio donde el río se encuentra con la bahía, donde hay venados, conejos, pinos y bayas, se fundó la misión Santa Cruz en 1791.

El gobernador estableció el pueblo de Branciforte en 1796, al otro lado del río de donde estaba la misión. El pueblo se llenó de malhechores de México que fueron a dar allí en vez de ir a la cárcel.

Estos causaron terribles problemas en la misión. Más tarde, la lluvia y el viento casi destruyen el edificio.

El Padre Quintana fue asesinado en su cama en la misión. En 1834 secularizaron la misión y luego dos terremotos destruyeron lo que quedaba. En 1931 se construyó una iglesia más pequeña que aún existe.

Nuestra Señora de la Soledad

The Lonesome Mission

This mission has a "lonely name." It means our lady of solitude or all alone. It is one of the names of the Virgin Mary. The Native Americans who joined the mission called themselves "soledad." 30 priests were in and out of that mission in 44 years. Do you think so many priests left because they were lonesome? Farming, however, was successful.

Two terrible epidemics killed or drove off lots of Native Americans. There were some terrible floods, and finally the mission collapsed.

Father Sarria, the mission's last priest kept the mission going alone for seven years. Do you think he got lonesome? He died in 1835.

The Lonesome Mission
La misión solitaria

La misión solitaria

Esta misión lleva un "nombre solitario:" Nuestra Señora de la Soledad, o sea sola. Este es uno de los nombres de la Virgen María. Los indígenas americanos que se unieron a la misión se pusieron el nombre de "soledad." En 44 años hubo 30 curas que llegaron y se fueron de esa misión. ¿Crees que tantos curas se fueron a causa de sentirse muy solos? Sin embargo, la agricultura sí tuvo éxito.

Dos terribles epidemias mataron o ahuyentaron a muchos indígenas. Hubo algunas inundaciones terribles, y finalmente la misión se derrumbó.

El padre Sarria, el último cura de la misión, la mantuvo activa por siete años. ¿Crees que se sintió muy solo? Murío en 1835.

San José

A Musical Mission

For 27 years, Father Narcisco Durán, a very capable person, was in charge of the mission. He directed many different activities. He wrote, taught music, and his Native American orchestra became famous and played European instruments.

Father Durán directed construction of a fine irrigation system. The mission became second only to San Gabriel in farming. There were 6,673 converts over time.

Father Durán also handled perhaps the biggest problem of all, attacks by Native Americans from the inland valley.

A Musical Mission
Una misión musical

Una misión musical

Por 27 años, el padre Narcisco Durán, una persona muy hábil, estaba a cargo de la misión. Dirigía las diferentes actividades. Escribía, daba clases de música, y su orquesta se hizo famosa y tocaba instrumentos europeos.

El padre Durán dirigió la construcción de un excelente sistema de riego. La misión llego a ser la segunda misión en la agricultura, después de la misión de San Gabriel. Con el tiempo, hubo 6.673 neófitos.

El padre Durán también tenía que proteger la misión contra los ataques de los indígenas del valle del interior. Este era quizas el problema más grave de la misión.

San Juan Bautista

The Seven Tongued Priest

This 15th mission was built in a beautiful spot over the Gabilan Mountains near the Salinas Valley.

Native Americans from the north, south, east and west joined the mission. Together, over the years, they worked and prayed. Father Arroyo de La Cuesta was the leader here for many years. He was very good at languages.

Father Cuesta learned to speak in all seven of the Native American lanugages used at this mission. He was able to preach, to pray and to talk to all of the neophytes in their native tongues for he was the seven tongued priest of Mission San Juan Bautista.

The Seven Tongued Priest
El cura de siete lenguas

El cura de siete lenguas

Esta 15ª misión se construyó en un lindo sitio en las montañas Gavilán cerca del valle de Salinas.

Indígenas del norte, sur, este y oeste se unieron a la misión. Con el tiempo, trabajaron y rezaron juntos. El padre Arroyo de La Cuesta fue un líder aquí por muchos años. Tenía mucha facilidad para los idiomas.

El padre aprendió a hablar todos los siete idiomas de los indígenas de la misión. Podía predicar, rezar y hablar con todos los neófitos en sus propias lenguas, pues era el cura de siete lenguas de las misión San Juan Bautista.

San Miguel Arcángel

The Mission With the Biggest Bell

This mission was the third of four founded in 1797. A big crowd of Native Americans came to the celebration. Fifteen children were baptized then. In fewer than ten years there were at least 1,000 neophytes.

The mission was founded at the fork of two rivers where the soil is very fertile.

It was a success. Wool, grain, cloth and leather were stored there but were burned up in a fire which also destroyed some buildings.

In 1888, long after the mission period, a 2,000 pound bell was made of bells from other missions. It rings to call people to the parish church, which Mission San Miguel has become.

The Mission With the Biggest Bell
La misión de la campana más grande

La misión de la campana más grande

Esta misión fue la tercera de cuatro misiónes fundadas en 1797. Una multitud de indígenas llegaron a la celebración. Entonces bautizaron a quince niños. En menos de diez años había por lo menos 1.000 neófitos.

Fundaron la misión en la confluencia de dos ríos donde la tierra es muy fértil.

Fue un éxito. Almacenaban lana, cereales, tela y cuero allí pero todo se quemó en un incendio que también destruyó algunos edificios.

En 1888, mucho tiempo después de la época de las misiónes, construyeron una campana de 2.000 libras, compuesta de las campanas de otras misiónes. Tocan la campana para llamar a la gente a la iglesia de la parroquia, que hoy día se conoce con el nombre la misión de San Miguel.

San Fernando Rey de España

The "Long Building" Mission

This was the fourth mission founded in 1797 and was built a day's travel from Los Angeles. The land was a gift to the mission by a Spanish settler because of its perfect location.

A small church was constructed within two months when 40 neophytes were in the mission.

The "Long Building" was built to give travelers from mission to mission a place to rest overnight. It grew to 243 feet and two stories. It is the largest adobe building in California.

The "Long Building" Mission
La misión del "edificio largo."

La misión del "edificio largo."

Esta misión fue la cuarta fundada en 1797 y la construyeron a un día de viaje de Los Angeles. Un colonizador español regaló el terreno por ser una ubicación perfecta.

Después de dos meses, cuando había 40 neófitos en las misión, ya habían construido una pequeña iglesia.

Construyeron el "edificio largo" para darles a los viajeros un lugar donde pasar la noche cuando iban de misión a misión. El edificio creció a 243 pies y era de dos pisos. Es el edificio de adobe más grande de California.

San Luis Rey de Francia

King of the Missions

This mission was founded very late. Many Native Americans wanted to join. The number of acres, sheep, cattle, horses and the size of the Indian Village became the largest. Father Peyri, the priest in charge for 33 years was able to do many things.

He drew the plans and watched over the construction of many of the buildings. He developed the water system, the laundry, baths, pools, and gardens. The church building was started in 1811, finished in 1815. It did not suffer in the 1812 earthquake. Father Peyri left the mission in 1832.

Over the years since 1846 the mission fell apart little by little. It has been rebuilt and is beautiful today.

King of the Missions
Rey de las misiones

Rey de las misiones

Esta misión se fundó muy tarde. Muchos indígenas querían pertenecer. Por la cantidad de acres, ovejas, ganado, caballos y por el tamaño de la aldea indígena, esta misión se convirtió en la más grande. El padre Peyri, el cura que estuvo a cargo por 33 años, pudo lograr muchas cosas.

Dibujó los planos y vigiló la construcción de muchos de los edificios. Construyó el sistema de agua, la lavandería, los baños, las albercas y los jardines. Empezaron a construir la iglesia en 1811 y la terminaron en 1815. Esta no sufrió daños en el terremoto de 1812. El padre Peyri se fue de la misión en 1832.

Después de 1846, con los años la misión se cayó a pedazos poco a poco. La han reconstruido y hoy día es muy bella.

Santa Inez

The Mission With the Danish Accent

The last of the Southern California Missions was built in a beautiful valley. Over recent years the Danish town of Solvang has grown up around the mission.

It started out well in 1804. 200 Native Americans joined right away and 20 babies were baptized. In a few years there was trouble.

Some of the buildings were ruined in the earthquake of 1812. A Spanish guard beat a neophyte in the 1820s and his friends were so angry they set a few buildings on fire. The church started to burn accidentally and the Native Americans put it out.

The mission is in good shape now and worth a visit.

The Mission With the Danish Accent
La misión del acento danés

La misión del acento danés

La última misión del sur de California fue construida en un lindo valle. En los años recientes, el pueblo danés de Solvang ha crecido alrededor de la misión.

Todo empezó muy bien en 1804. 100 indígenas se unieron imediatamente y se bautizaron 20 bebés. Después de pocos años hubo problemas.

El terremoto de 1812 destruyó algunos de los edifícios. Un guarda español golpeó a un neófito en la década de 1829 y los amigos de éste se enfurecieron tanto que incendiaron algunos de los edificios. La iglesia se empezó a quemar accidentalmente y los indígenas apagaron el fuego.

Hoy día la misión se encuentra en buenas condiciones y vale la pena visitarla.

San Rafael Arcángel

The 10 Mile Health Plan

The hospital mission San Rafael was founded across the bay from Mission Dolores. The weather was protected by the mountains. Hundreds of neophytes had died or were sick from the cold, foggy San Francisco climate.

Its warm dry weather helped the crops and livestock, too. In 1823 it became a real mission, not just a hospital. 113 years later the Golden Gate Bridge was built and millions of people have since enjoyed the warm summer weather just north of San Francisco.

The 10 Mile Health Plan
El plan de salud de 10 millas

El plan de salud de 10 millas

La misión hospital San Rafael se fundó al otro lado de la bahía de donde está la misión Dolores. Las montañas protegen el clima. Cientos de neófitos habían muerto o estaban enfermos del clima frío y neblinoso de San Francisco.

El clima templado y seco de San Rafael ayudó las cosechas y el ganado. En 1823 se convirtó en una verdadera misión, no sólo un hospital. 113 años más tarde se construyó el puente Golden Gate y desde entonces, millones de personas disfrutan del clima de verano templado justo al norte de San Francisco.

San Francisco de Solano

"Russians Keep Out"

The Russians built Fort Ross on the northern California coast in mission times. The Spanish wanted to build a mission to keep them from the south.

A young priest named Father Jose Altimira had just come to Mission Dolores from Spain. He wanted to close two missions, build a huge one and make all the Indians Catholic. The governor agreed, the church officials said, "No way, Jose." They let the mission at Sonoma be built but no missions were closed.

General Vallejo took over the mission in 1835, built the chapel in 1849. The Russians soon left Fort Ross.

"Prohibida la entrada a los rusos"

Los rusos construyeron el fuerte Ross en las costa del norte de California durante la época de las misiones. Los españoles querían construir una misión para evitar que entraran los rusos al sur.

Un cura joven que se llamaba el padre José Altimira acababa de llegar de España a la misión Dolores. Quería cerrar dos misiones, construir una grande y convertir a todos los indígenas al catolicismo. El gobernador estuvo de acuerdo, pero los oficiales de la iglesia dijeron que de ninguna manera. Permitieron que se construyera la misión en Sonoma pero no se cerró ninguna otra misión.

El general Vallejo se apoderó de la misión en 1835, y construyó la capilla en 1849. Pronto los rusos se fueron del fuerte Ross.

"Russians Keep Out"
"Prohibida la entrada a los rusos"

Exploración - Colón

Un hecho histórico en verso - - -

Muchos años han pasado
Que navegó Colón del otro lado.

Vino derecho a un "mundo nuevo."
Y causó, claro está, un gran revuelo.

Desde entonces el mundo dio un cambio.
Entre los dos mundos, ¡Vaya intercambio!

Otros exploradores y pobladores también
Siguieron a Colón para mal o para bien.

Del "nuevo mundo" al "viejo" fueron maíz y papas,
tomates y chiles; nació la pizza en varias etapas.

Caballos, cabras y caña de azucar trajeron consigo,
y cebada, y avena, centeno y trigo.

Mencionaremos sólo unos pocos.
De los que vinieron del "viejo mundo" al otro.

Ya tarde, Alta California fundaron un día
Levantó la neibla y se vio la bahía.

En el año de 1769,
El Padre Serra bien se mueve.

Dedicó la primera misión, sin embargo.
Los fraciscanos le hacen este encargo.

Los fundadores de las misiones trajeron portentos
Que incluían mulas que corrían como el viento.

Comerciaron con los indígenas de aquel lugar,
y vieron por vez primera un ciervo, sin dudar.

En el intercambio, no gustó una cosa, y no son maldades,
Del "viejo mundo" al "nuevo" trajeron enfermedades.

Exploration - Columbus

A factual account in verse - - -

Columbus sailed the ocean vast,
And many a year has long since passed.

He sailed right to a brand "new world"
And saying the least, caused quite a whirl.

From that time on, the whole world changed
'Tween these worlds – WOW! What an exchange.

Other explorers and settlers, too
Followed Columbus and what a "to-do!"

From "New World" to "old" went potatoes and corn,
Tomatoes and chiles; the pizza was born.

The horse, and goats and sugar cane, sweet,
And barley, oats and rye and wheat,

Just to name a very few,
Went from the "Old World" to the "New."

Alta California was founded late
Because fog covered the "Golden Gate" (?)

The year was 1769
Father Serra was feeling fine.

He dedicated the very first Mission,
The Franciscans to him, gave that commission.

The Missions' founders brought great wonders
Including mules that sounded like thunder.

They traded treats with the Natives here
And probably saw their very first deer.

In trade, one thing sure didn't please,
From "Old World" to "New" they carried disease.

---Barbara Linse

California

California Map

Add any number of details to the "Blank Map."

Photo copy a map for every California Map Experience.

You and your class might want to enlarge it for a big class-map.

Each girl and boy may use many maps.

Use the map:

For showing the natural regions as: mountains, valleys, deserts, lakes, rivers, and the ocean.

For showing county bounderies.

To show highways, and other roads.

To show important places in the Gold Rush Days.

To find and show explorer routes and dates.

To show what you have learned and what you need to learn.

Plan a trip, real or make believe to Hollywood, or Yosemite, or Tahoe. You will need to put in the necessary markings.

Show where the Russians settled.

For making a climate map.

For anything else you want to show and share.

For showing California colors:

such as make a wild flower map,
a forest and cactus map,
a sun and rain map,
a bird map showing shore birds as well as the Swallows at Mission San Juan Capistrano.

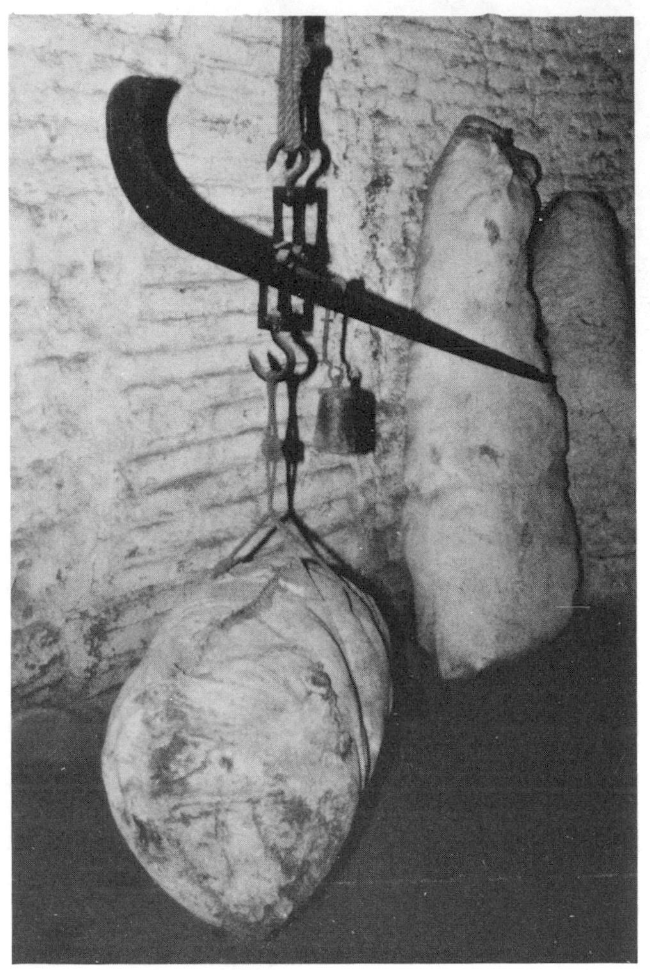

Mission Tools

Top Left - Scales used for weighing supplies and produce at the Missions.

Top Right - Inspecting a giant saw.

Bottom Left - Huge pot, however, it is now safe for these visiting children.

Humanizing Historical Characters

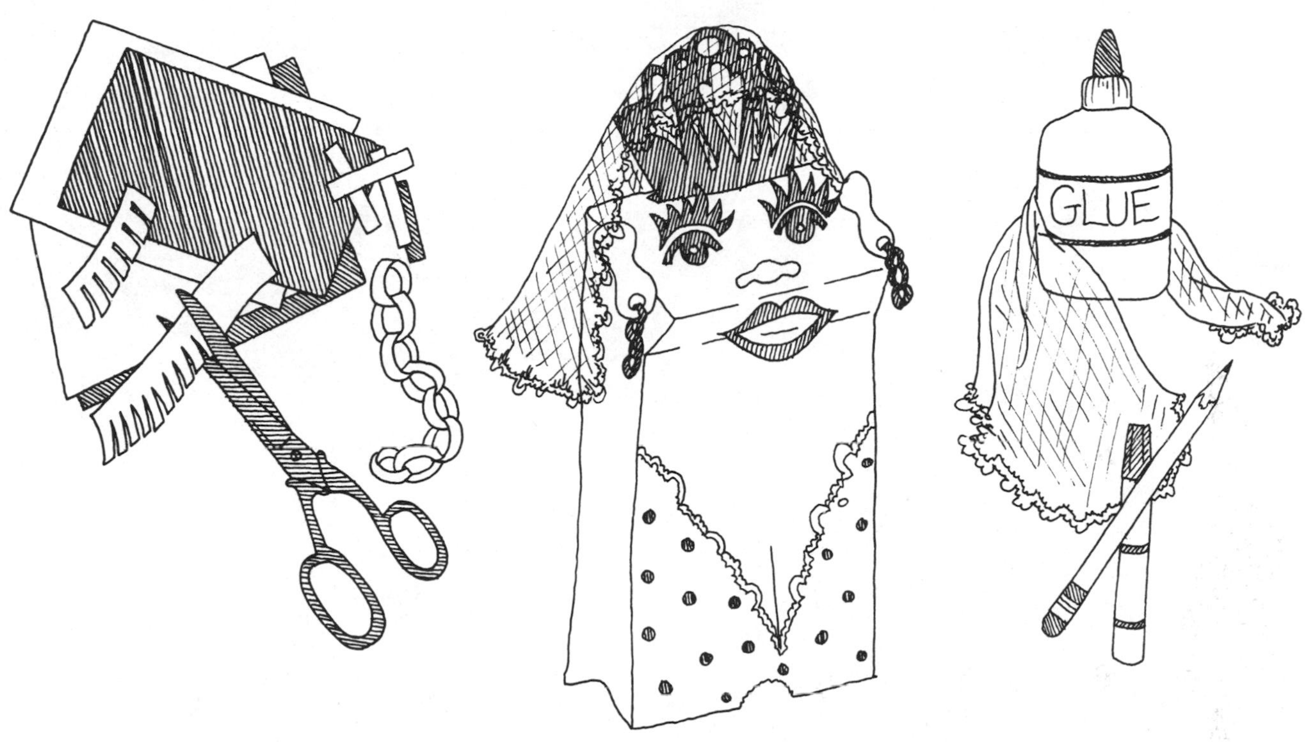

PAPER BAG PUPPET

Use lunch-size paper bag for best hand manipulation. The fold becomes the mouth.

Materials
- Lunch bags
- Scissors
- Pretty scraps
- Glue
- Crayons
- Pencils

SOCK PUPPET I

Cut toe out of socks.
Sew oval insert into toe area.
Decorate as shown in illustration.

SOCK PUPPET II

Stuff "foot" of socks.
Insert cardboard cylinder.
Tie or use rubber band to keep in place.
Decorate as shown in illustration.

Materials
- Socks
- Scissors
- Decorative scraps
- Needle
- Thread
- Glue

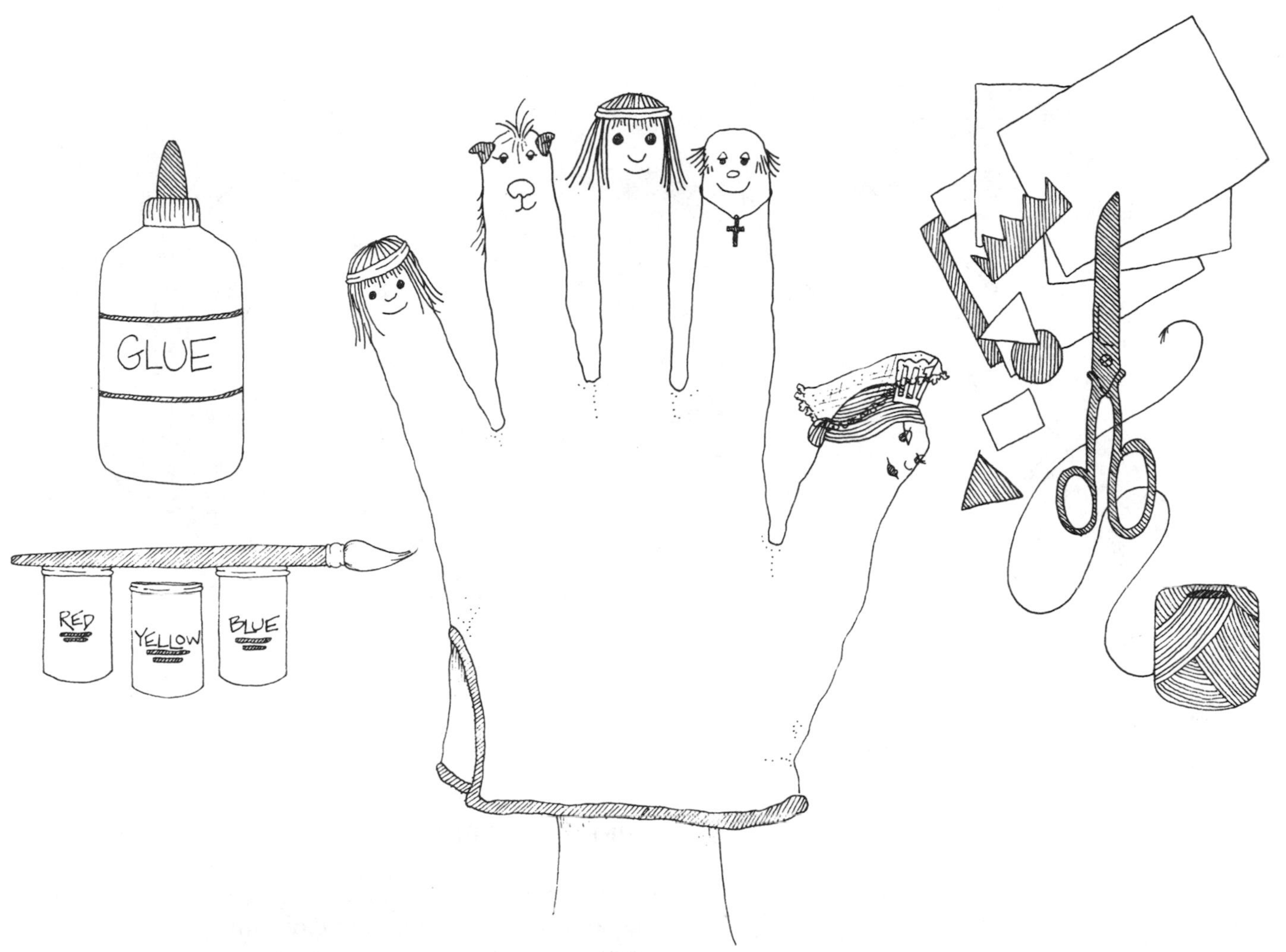

GLOVE FINGER PUPPET

Use a whole glove or cut off fingers of glove for a one-at-a-time puppet.

Materials — Cloth glove
— Pretty scraps
— Paint
— Scissors
— Glue

PAPER PLATE PUPPET

Fold a paper plate and staple in the center. Fold and sew a large piece of cloth into a "sleeve" and attach to the plate with glue or tape. Finish and decorate.

Materials — Bags
— Scissors
— Staples
— Glue
— Colored paper
— Cloth
— Needle and thread

LIGHT GLOBE PUPPET

Cover the light globe with vaseline; place in a paper cylinder and onto the bottle for easy work. Build up and strip with maché layers but don't cover the bottle. Remove from the base. If you wish, remove the glass by giving the head a hard crack then carefully cutting the head and shaking the glass into a bag. Retape head with maché or masking tape. Decorate the puppet and dress it simply with paper or cloth.

Materials — Glove
— Bottle
— Cylinder
— Maché mash and strips
— Decorative scraps
— Scissors
— Cloth
— Glue

PUPPET STAGES

Make puppet stages using big boxes or upsidedown tables, as shown. Put on a bit of the play given here; better yet, write one of your own!

Materials
- Box or table
- Cloth

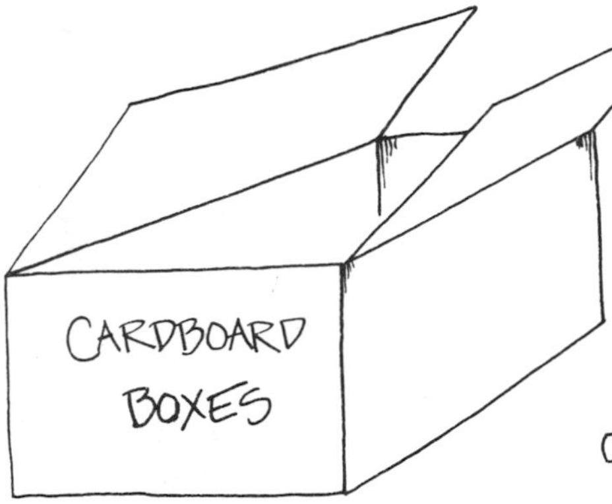

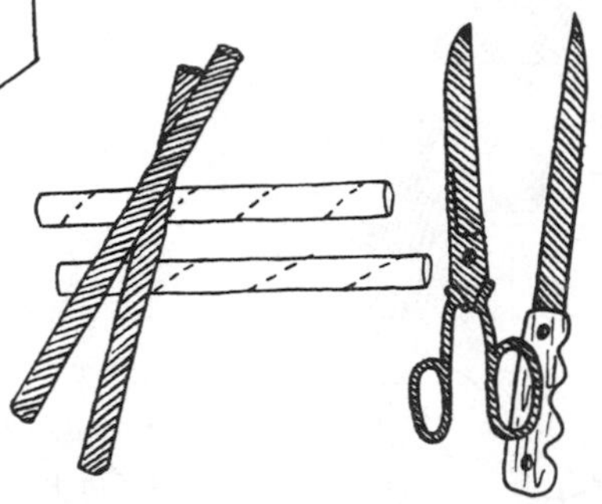

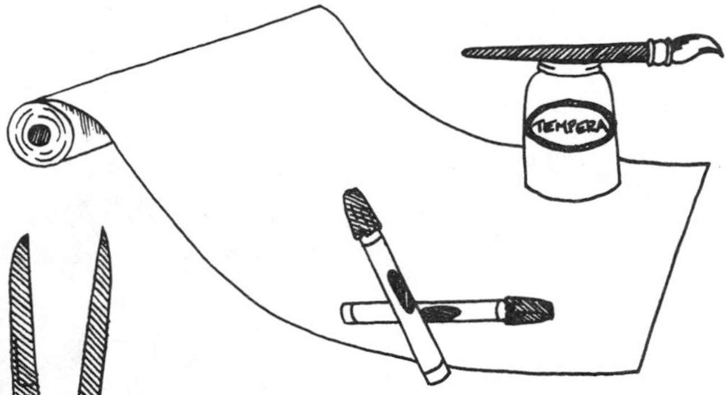

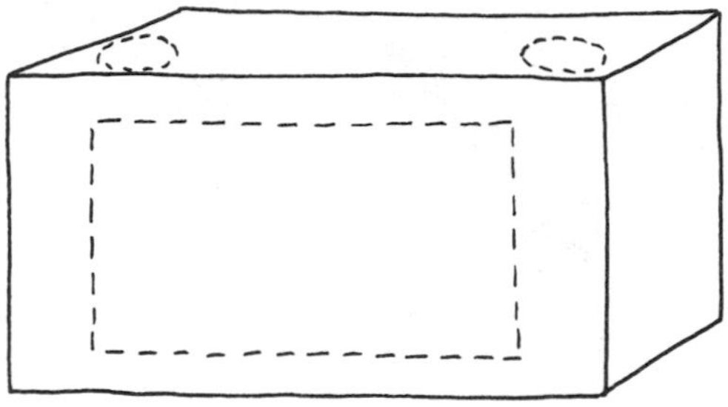

CREATE A MOVIE OR TELEVISION SHOW

Make the sequential story frames on a roll of shelf or cut down butcher paper. A cardboard box with a viewing hole cut in front and roling holes on top will work well. Dowel sticks cut taller than the box or cardboard cylinders make fine rollers.

Materials — Large box
— Dowel sticks
— Cardboard cylinders
— Shelf paper
— Paint or crayons or felt pen markers

PAPER PLATE MASK

Fasten string to each side of paper plate (as shown); decorate to give your desired personality to the mask.

Materials — Paper plate
— String
— Glue
— Colored paper
— Decorative scraps
— Scissors
— Paint

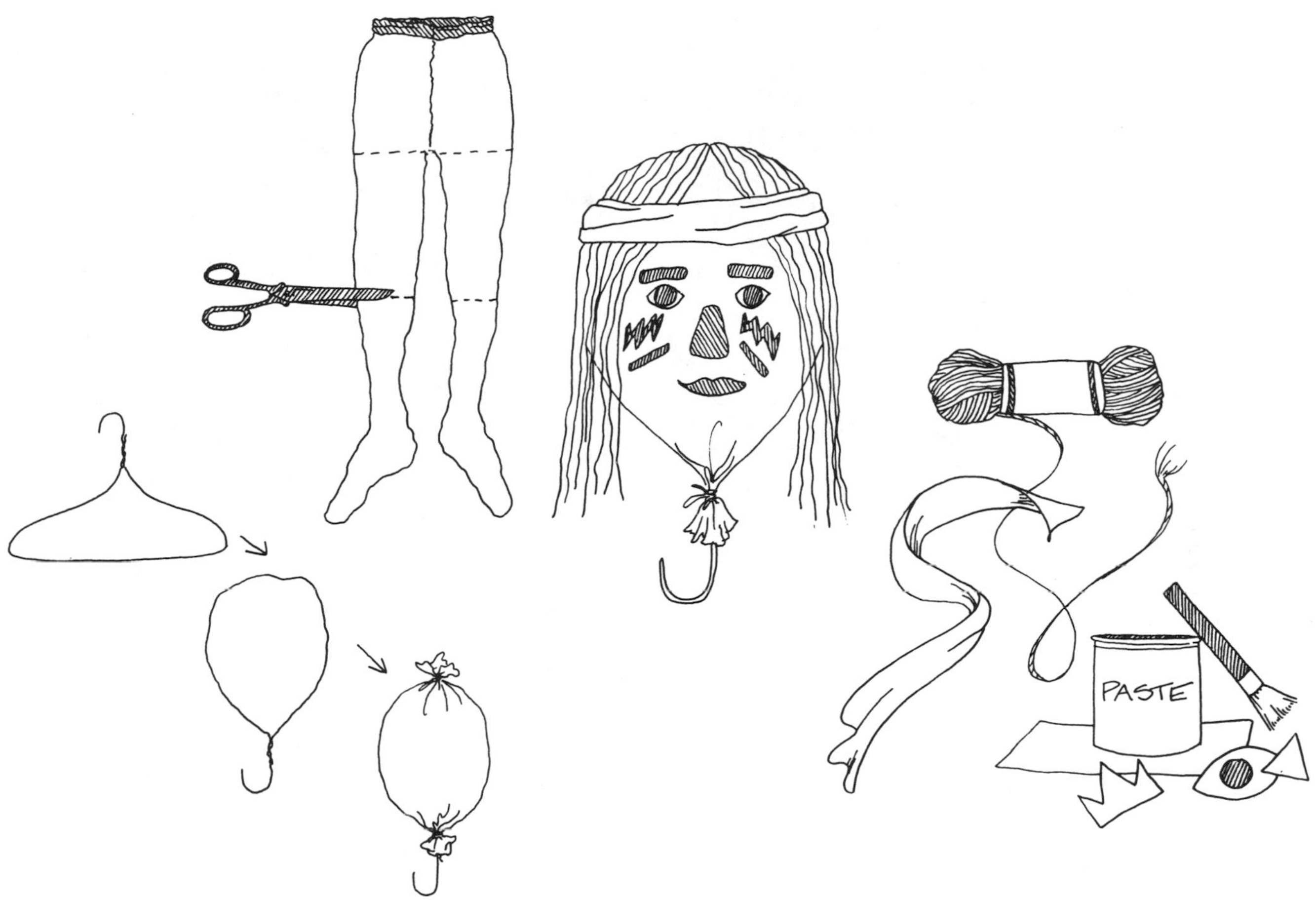

COAT HANGER MASK

Cut stocking off.
Shape wire coat hanger into a circle.
Stretch the stocking and tie as shown.
Decorate with paper and material.
Use it to hide behind.

Materials — Panty hose
— Wire hanger
— Decorative scraps
— Scissors
— Paste or glue

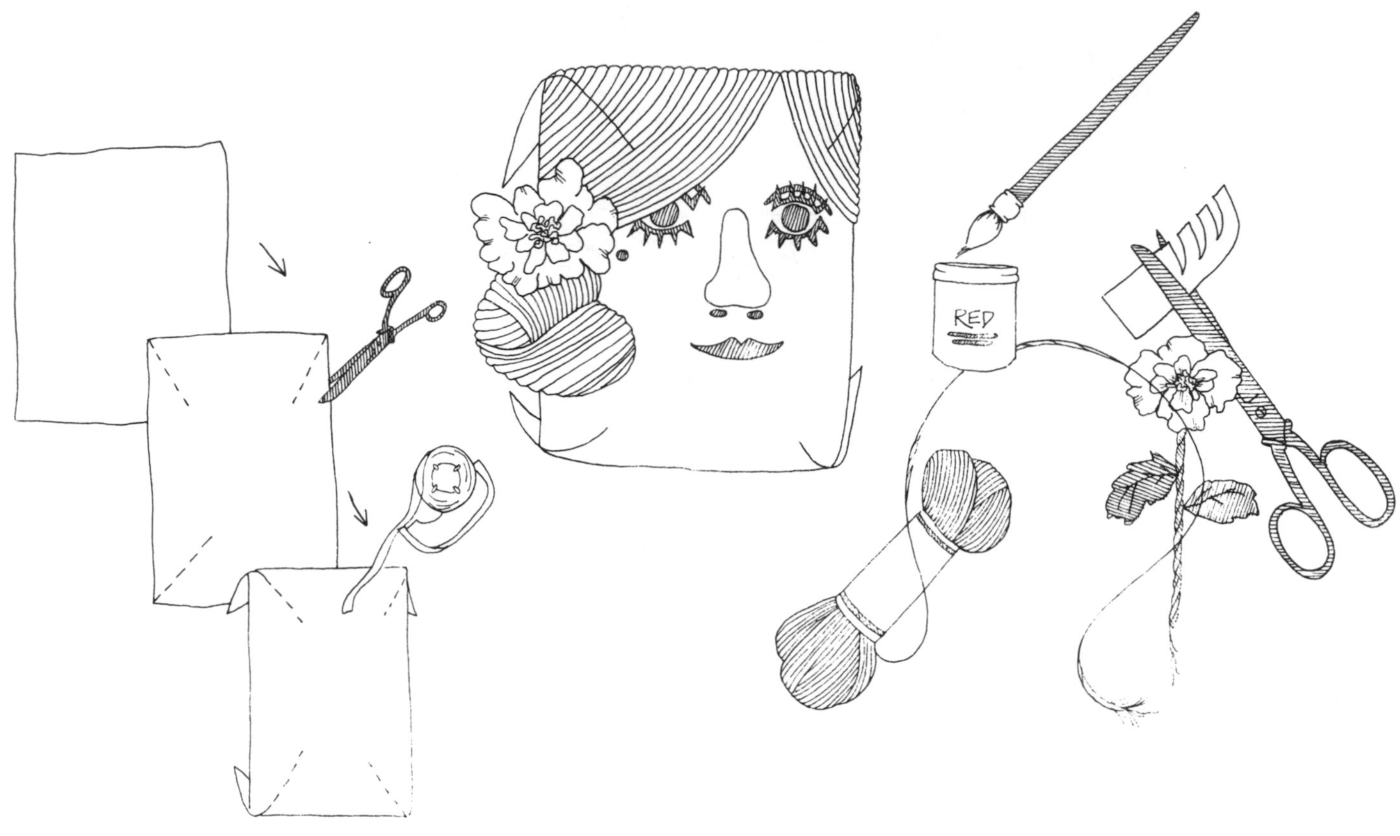

FOLDED PAPER MASK

Draw slashed lines.
Cut and tape.
Use remaining lines as folding guides to give shape to the mask.

Materials – Paper
– Scissors
– Decorative scraps
– Glue

The California Missions

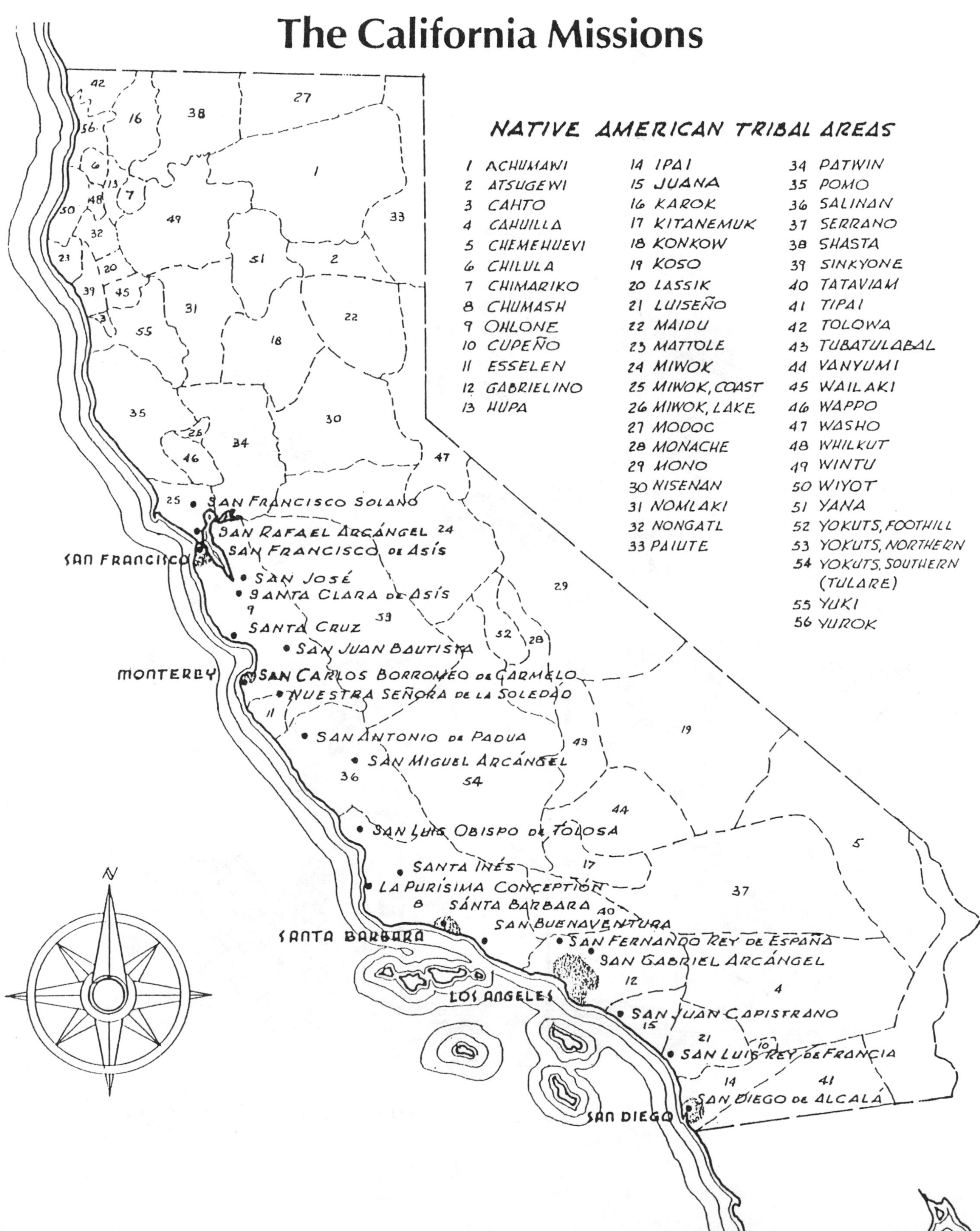
NATIVE AMERICAN TRIBAL AREAS
1 ACHUMAWI
2 ATSUGEWI
3 CAHTO
4 CAHUILLA
5 CHEMEHUEVI
6 CHILULA
7 CHIMARIKO
8 CHUMASH
9 OHLONE
10 CUPEÑO
11 ESSELEN
12 GABRIELINO
13 HUPA
14 IPAI
15 JUANA
16 KAROK
17 KITANEMUK
18 KONKOW
19 KOSO
20 LASSIK
21 LUISEÑO
22 MAIDU
23 MATTOLE
24 MIWOK
25 MIWOK, COAST
26 MIWOK, LAKE
27 MODOC
28 MONACHE
29 MONO
30 NISENAN
31 NOMLAKI
32 NONGATL
33 PAIUTE
34 PATWIN
35 POMO
36 SALINAN
37 SERRANO
38 SHASTA
39 SINKYONE
40 TATAVIAM
41 TIPAI
42 TOLOWA
43 TUBATULABAL
44 VANYUMI
45 WAILAKI
46 WAPPO
47 WASHO
48 WHILKUT
49 WINTU
50 WIYOT
51 YANA
52 YOKUTS, FOOTHILL
53 YOKUTS, NORTHERN
54 YOKUTS, SOUTHERN (TULARE)
55 YUKI
56 YUROK
SAN FRANCISCO SOLANO
SAN RAFAEL ARCÁNGEL
SAN FRANCISCO DE ASÍS
SAN FRANCISCO
SAN JOSÉ
SANTA CLARA DE ASÍS
SANTA CRUZ
SAN JUAN BAUTISTA
MONTEREY
SAN CARLOS BORROMEO DE CARMELO
NUESTRA SEÑORA DE LA SOLEDAD
SAN ANTONIO DE PADUA
SAN MIGUEL ARCÁNGEL
SAN LUIS OBISPO DE TOLOSA
SANTA INÉS
LA PURISIMA CONCEPTIÓN
SANTA BARBARA
SAN BUENAVENTURA
SANTA BARBARA
SAN FERNANDO REY DE ESPAÑA
SAN GABRIEL ARCÁNGEL
LOS ANGELES
SAN JUAN CAPISTRANO
SAN LUIS REY DE FRANCIA
SAN DIEGO DE ALCALÁ
SAN DIEGO
N

Mission San Diego de Alcalá
george kuska

San Diego de Alcalá

(First Mission, July 16, 1769)

The first mission was named for Saint Didacus, who was born near Seville, Spain around 1400 of humble parents. He was a hermit, a Franciscan missionary to the Canary Islands, a miraculous healer in Rome, and head of the infirmary of the University of Alcalá in Castille, Spain where he died in 1463.

Our civilization in California was born with founding this Mission. Like most births, it wasn't easy. Two overland parties and three ships were sent from Lower California to "Occupy and fortify San Diego and Monterey for God and the King of Spain," as ordered by Carlos III. One ship disappeared in a trial voyage before the expedition even started. Another, the *San Carlos,* was blown off course and the crew incapacitated with scurvy before they reached San Diego harbor. The overland parties tried to take too much livestock.

This travel weary band of survivors gathered to implement their bold and unique plan. Father Junipero Serra blessed the cross and celebrated High Mass in the chapel. The date was July 16, 1769 and the spiritual conquest of California was underway.

Sickness, death, and near starvation reduced the survivors from about ninety to fewer than thirty men. The mission could not become self-sufficient and at one time Governor Portolá ordered it abandoned unless relief arrived in the next few days.

The California Natives did not appreciate that all of this was for their salvation. None were to be seen at the founding ceremonies. However, in just a few years, the Fathers were converting enough California Natives that their leaders were afraid their tribal way of life would be destroyed. They plotted to drive the foreigners out of their land. On a night in November 1775, an army of hundreds of California Natives attacked the Mission with spears, bows and arrows. Nine men and two boys were the entire white population at the Mission when the attack came. Father Luis Jayme rushed out to talk to the army. He was one of the three defenders killed that night, the first Father martyred in California. The buildings were all burned. The California Natives delayed the Mission movement with their attack.

The Mission prospered in the following years and had the fourth largest congregation in the Mission chain before secularization. At present it meets the pastoral needs of 2,000 families that belong to the mission parish.

To reduce the influence of the Presidio soldiers on the converts, the mission was moved six miles up the valley in 1774. A new church of adobe and wood was built. It was the one destroyed in the California Native attack. In 1780 a second, larger church was constructed and a tile roof added in 1792. An earthquake in 1803 almost completely destroyed it.

The belfry is one of the more interesting features of the building. Known as a campanario, it is composed of only one wall as compared to four walls in a bell tower. The front wall, or fachada, is also known as an espadaña. It is the raised gable or false front that was used to make the building seem larger.

There is a continual restoration program at San Diego de Alcalá. The original copper baptismal font has recently been added to the collection of artifacts.

Mission San Diego Alcalá
10818 San Diego Mission Road
San Diego , CA 92108
619-283-7319

Historic site museum.
Activities: Located in first Rectory and residence of Juipero Serra, collections include Native American baskets, Spanish colonial and early American artifacts, ecclesiastical objects, and archival materials. Tote-a-tape tour. Booklet and brochures.
Hours: 9-5, daily; adults, $1; children under 12, no charge
Contact: Mary C. Whelan, Curator

Mission San Carlos - Carmel
george kuska

San Carlos Borromeo de Carmelo

(Second Mission, June 3, 1770)

How the Mission Got Its Name

Saint Charles Borromeo is the namesake of the second mission. Charles was born in Italy in 1538 and died in 1584. His uncle was Pope Pius IV. He was the first great leader of the Counter-Reformation.

Two days after he arrived at Monterey Bay, Father Serra consecrated the ground and celebrated mass under the same oak tree Viscaino used 168 years before. The natives were friendly. The natural beauty of the area and the climate all impressed Father Serra. This Mission became his headquarters for administration of the other Missions.

The first buildings were wooden structures because of the abundance of pine and cypress trees. However, the fathers were prompted to move the Mission away from the un-Christian conduct of the soldiers, to an area with more farm land at the mouth of Carmel Valley, its present location.

The first adobe church was started here in 1774, under the direction of Father Serra himself. The present stone church, a dream of Father Serra, was begun in 1793. Father Lasuen brought a master stone mason, Manuel Estevan Ruiz, from Mexico for the work. The Carmel area has a soft white stone that is easy to work. It hardens and turns a darker yellow when exposed to the air.

Although it was the administrative headquarters of the Missions it never had as many Indians as the others.

The architecture is more satisfying and unique than any in the Mission chain. The two towers are not "twin" but each very distinctive, one topped with a Moorish dome. The star window is simply fascinating.

In spite of its importance, religiously, architecturally and economically, it deteriorated rapidly after secularization. Before long it was a ruin. Attempts to restore it were started in 1881. A pitched roof was added to protect the walls, but it was out of character with the architecture. In 1934, it was removed, and an accurate restoration has taken place since.

The Mission at Carmel today is a parish church, and a visit to it is one of the great experiences we can have in reliving this part of our history.

Something Special

Mission San Carlos Borromeo
3080 Rio Road
Carmel, CA 93921

Archives and/or manuscript repository and Spanish era mission.
Activities: Hold the Harry Downie Collection of photos, source documents, and books related to early California and the mission. Use at the discretion of the curator. Write for an appointment. Gift shop.
Hours: 9:30 - 4:30, Mon-Sat; 10:30-4:30, Sun.
Contact: Richard Menn, Curator

Mission San Antonio de Padua
george kuska

San Antonio de Padua

(Third Mission, July 14, 1771)

How the Mission Got Its Name

Saint Anthony, patron saint of the third mission was born in Lisbon, Portugal in 1195 and died in 1231. He was a famous preacher and a miracle worker who became patron to the poor. Believers pray to St. Anthony for the return of lost articles. He is buried at Padova (Padua) in northern Italy.

If it weren't for the military presence in Hunter-Liggett, a visit to this Mission in a beautiful oak-studded valley in the Santa Lucia Mountains is almost like going back in time. Father Serra founded San Antonio on the route Portola took between San Diego and Monterey, the first Mission not on the coast.

The Indians were friendly, but were not too anxious to accept Christianity. However, the Mission continued to grow. An adobe chapel was built in 1782 with a tile roof. This is the first example of the use of the material that became a trade mark of Mission architecture to later generations.

Water was necessary before the Mission could really prosper, so eventually a complex water system that dammed the San Antonio River was developed. The system of reservoirs, settling ponds, and conduits were so well developed that the ranchers used them long after the Mission had fallen into ruin. A water-powered gristmill was built for grinding grain into flour that was justly famous throughout the Mission chain.

The present church was started in 1810. Its architecture is unusual and pleasing. It is an adobe building with a facade of decorative clay brick that also serves as a companario for three bells.

The Mission prospered until it counted 1,300 Indians and 17,491 head of livestock. After secularization, Governor Pio Pico offered to sell the disintegrated Mission but nobody wanted to buy it.

First attempts to restore the buildings began in 1903 but the earthquake of 1906 caused the project to be abandoned. Current restoration started in 1948 and is continuing.

Something Special

Mission San Antonio de Padua
Mission Creek Road (P. O. Box 803)
Jolon, CA 93928
408-385-4478

Archives and/or manuscript repository and a restored Spanish era mission.
Activities: Restored between 1948-1949, the mission is located within Fort Hunter-Liggett Military Reservation. Collections relate to the mission history and restoration and advance permission to use is necessary. Horizontal grist mill is on grounds. Gift shop.
Hours: 9:30 - 4:30, daily
Contact: Leo Sprietsma, OFM, Director

Missio San Gabriel
george kuska

San Gabriel Arcángel

(Fourth Mission, September 8, 1771)

The Archangel Gabriel, patron saint of the fourth mission, is one of three angels named in the Bible. He is mentioned twice in the Book of Daniel, announced the birth of John the Baptist and the birth of Jesus.

Mission San Gabriel is completely surrounded by metropolitan growth. Where it is possible to visualize the third Mission, San Antonio, as it was in the eighteenth century, it is impossible with San Gabriel. Although the church building itself survived secularization and is in a more original condition than other Missions, you can not even imagine the vast agricultural lands controlled by the Mission.

There are several reasons for the success of San Gabriel. The Mission lands were very fertile, favored by a gentle climate and with available water. The fathers were hard working and resourceful over a period of time. The site was located at the cross-roads of three major land routes, from Mexico, from the east, and from the north.

The Indians were friendly until a soldier interrupted the harmony and a chief was killed. It took a while for the Fathers to reestablish a good feeling with the Indians. Eventually, the Mission was a spiritual and material success. It was so successful with agriculture products that it is known as the "Mother of California Agriculture".

The present church was begun in 1794, and finished in 1806. The thirty foot high walls are of stone to the windows, then of brick with stucco as the finish. The original roof was vaulted stone. An earthquake forced a change in design when the roof cracked and was replaced with a low pitched timber gable in 1803. Its unique Moorish design is inspired by the cathedral at Cordova, Spain where Father Cruzado had studied.

The prosperity and lands were lost during secularization, but the church was never completely deserted. The United States restored the property to the Catholic Church with the church still intact. It served as a parish church from 1859 to 1908, when it was taken over by the Cloretan Fathers. It has been refurbished and had excellent care since that time.

San Gabriel Mission Museum
537 W. Mission Drive
San Gabriel, CA 91776
818-282-5191

Archives and/or manuscript repository and Spanish mission musuem.
Activities: Located on the site of the fourth of the 21 California Missions, founded by 1771. Guided tours, education programs, permanent exhibitions.
Hours: In 1992 closed for renovation.
Contact: Rev. Gary E. Smith, C. M. F. Director

Mission San Luis Obispo de Tolosa
george kuska

San Luis Obispo de Tolosa

(Fifth Mission, September 1, 1772)

How the Mission Got Its Name

Saint Louis, Bishop of Toulouse, is the namesake of the fifth mission. Louis was born in 1274 in southern France, and he died at the age of 23 in 1297. His father was King of Naples, his grandfather was King Stephen V of Hungary, and his uncle was Saint Louis IX of France. He, with his two younger brothers, held hostage in Barcelona for seven years in exchange for their father who was captured in a naval battle. During that time, Franciscan friars instructed him. He was consecrated Bishop of Toulouse a year before he died of a fever.

Father Serra founded this Mission while he was on his way to San Diego to hasten the supplies from Mexico aboard the ships to Monterey. He selected a site not on the coast, but several miles inland surrounded by mountains, known as the "Valley of the Bears". Portola had named the valley on his first trip to Monterey because of so many grizzly bears in the area.

At least three times in the first years of the Mission, these bears were used for food when provisions ran low. One hunt, from San Antonio and Carmel to save the starving people, produced over 9,000 lbs. of bear meat. No wonder the grizzly bears became extinct in California.

The Indians were friendly to the newcomers because they had also received meat from the bear hunts by trading seeds. They gave the Fathers food, but were not anxious to join the Mission because they had more food. It wasn't until the Mission began producing corn and beans that they attracted converts.

Indians did attack the Mission on several occasions, enemies of some of the tribes who came to live there. They used burning arrows shot onto the thatched roofs, setting the buildings on fire. The Fathers were forced to make clay tile to roof the buildings. The idea was from San Antonio,but before long it was used in all the Missions.

The present church was completed in 1793, an adobe building with a clay tile roof. The facade, with three bells, was not completed until 1820.

The Mission became a parish church after secularization and is still one. The adobe walls were covered with wood siding, the roof with wood shingles, and a wooden steeple was added to make it seem more like home to the settlers from the eastern United States. However, true restoration was started in 1933 to return it to its appearance today.

A city plaza has been developed in front of the church, so the area is filled with activity as it was during its glory days.

Something Special

Mission San Luis Obispo de Tolosa
728 Monterey Street (P. O. Box 1461)
San Luis Obispo, CA 93401
805-543-6850

Spanish era Mission and museum. Number of members: 12
Activities: Area, Chumash Indian, and mission artifacts. Yearly "Indian Art Festival."
Docent guided tour by appointment.
Hours: May - Sept: 9 - 5, daily; Oct - April: 10 - 4, daily
Contact: Mrs. Sally Minor, Curator and Gift Shop Manager

Mission Dolores
george kuska

San Francisco de Asís

(Sixth Mission, October 9, 1776)

How the Mission Got Its Name

Saint Francis of Assisi was chosen as the patron of the sixth mission. He was born in Assisi, Italy in 1182 and died in 1226. He was the son of a wealthy family but finally gave it up for the vows of poverty, obedience, and chastity; thereby starting the founding of the Franciscan Order. His appreciation of nature and all of God's creatures was unique and has had a profound effect on succeeding generations.

The Great San Francisco Bay was rather late in being discovered because the Golden Gate is a narrow entrance for such a large bay. Portola finally determined it was a great bay on his second trip north. Its strategic importance was immediately recognized and orders were issued to found two Missions and a presidio with a colony of families there without delay.

Thus started one of the most remarkable overland treks in western history. Juan Bautista de Anza led 240 settlers and about 1,000 domestic animals from Sonora, Mexico, to Mission San Xavier del Bac, along the Gila River to the Colorado, forded it to cross the desert, the mountains, and the coastal plain to Mission San Gabriel. Then on to Monterey and finally arriving at San Francisco Bay. He arrived with four more people than he started, with new born babies.

The Mission was founded near a stream that Anza named Arroyo de los Dolores (Our Lady of Sorrows) because it was her feast day. Even today, the Mission is known as Mission Dolores rather than its official name.

The Mission grew slowly. The land was too sandy for good crops. The Indians appreciated the food, shelter, and protection of the Mission, but they were also influenced by the immoralities of the presidio and lack of discipline in their neighboring tribes. They ran away from the Mission in great numbers at times. Sickness was a major factor in limiting the Indian population of the Mission. Measles epidemics in 1806 and 1826 were responsible for over 500 Indian deaths. 5,500 Indians died here during the Mission's 58 years of existence.

The present church was dedicated in 1791, an adobe building with redwood roof timbers lashed together with rawhide, and clay tile roof. Redwood was available for construction from Monterey north. Wooden pegs of manzanita were commonly used to connect timbers in structures. The facade of the building was not built until about 1810 when skilled masons were available in the area.

After secularization, the church was used for various purposes so it didn't fall into ruin. The church has been carefully preserved and faithfully kept. It survived the great earthquake of 1906 and even in its City location, it has a distinctive character all its own even today.

Something Special

Mission Dolores
3321 16th Street
San Francisco, CA 94114
415-621-8203

Activities: School groups can make tours.
Appointments needed for tours. which are given at 9:30 and 10:30, Tues. through Fri.
Ask about special programs such as fiestas given at the Basilica.
A gift shop is open daily from 9 to 4.

Mission San Juan Capistrano
george kuska

San Juan de Capistrano

(Seventh Mission, November 1, 1776)

The seventh mission was named after Saint John of Capistrano. John was born in1385 in Capistrano, a village in central Italy. He was of noble birth, studied law, and was named governor of the city. He organized a crusade against the then victorious Turks and turned them back at Belgrade. A short time after that victory, he died of a fever in 1456.

San Juan Capistrano was founded twice, the first time by Father Lasuen on October 30, 1775. Less than a week later, word arrived of the Indian uprising at San Diego. It was hastily abandoned and not founded again until Father Serra came a year later.

The Mission prospered immediately. The location near the sea had a mild climate, workable rich soil, water and friendly Indians. The Mission was the famous example of the hide and tallow trade that established a flourishing and profitable export to the eastern United States.

An adobe church was built, with the first section finished in 1777, a year after the founding of the Mission. It is the only one left existing in which Father Serra celebrated Mass. To us it becomes important as the oldest building in California, and is known as "Father Serra's Chapel".

Beginning in 1796, work was started on a huge stone church to be the most impressive building in the whole Mission chain. Isidor Aguilar, an expert stonemason from Mexico, was brought to oversee the construction. The church was under construction for nine years. The immense structure had seven masonry domes, an unusually elaborate stone treatment, vaulting over the sanctuary, and side arches along the nave. It was a most sophisticated design and construction.

The church was used for only six years when the devastating earthquake of December 1812, toppled the tower and destroyed the church. Forty Indians were killed in the tragedy. It was never rebuilt.

In 1833, the Mission was secularized. The chapel was used for a time as a hay barn, thus the roof was maintained and the walls protected.

Attempts to restore the Mission started in 1860, but they mainly destroyed part of what was left. In 1920, a truly effective restoration started. Today this is a popular tourist attraction and the remains of the great stone church are resplendent, even in ruins.

Mission Museum, San Juan Capistrano
Camino Capistrano and Ortego Highway (P. O. Box 313)
San Juan Capistrano, CA 92693
714-496-4720

Restored mission museum.
Activities: Gift shop, bookstore, film room, gardens, lecture and meeting room and archaelogical exhibits. Special events, living history, archaeological excavations by college students. Published 10 books and booklets on mission history and archaeology.
Hours: 8:30 - 7, daily
Contact: Nick Magalousis, Director

Mission Santa Clara de Asis
george kuska

Santa Clara de Asís

(Eighth Mission, January 12, 1777)

How the Mission Got Its Name

The eighth mission is the first whose patron is a female. Clara was born of noble parents in Assisi, Italy in 1194. She showed a pious attitude as a child, refused to marry, entered a convent, and eventually founded her own Order, the Poor Clares. It was based on the Order of Saint Francis, of the Franciscans. Clara died in 1253.

Santa Clara Mission was the second of the two ordered to be founded as protection for San Francisco Bay from the Russians or English. Some of the de Anza Colonists came to a new settlement nearby, the city of San José.

The site proved to be more difficult than ever imagined. At first, it was on the banks of the Guadalupe River, which flooded, two years later. It was moved to higher ground twice; then, in 1818, an earthquake destroyed the Mission. It was moved again, four times in all. The church was built and rebuilt a total of seven times, twice it was destroyed by fire.

In spite of these changing conditions, the Mission prospered and became one of the most successful in the whole chain of Missions. Santa Clara had very competent Fathers directing the Mission operations. It was also blessed with an ideal climate and rich deep soil for growing abundant crops. After 1784, it had a long period of prosperity and was second only to San Gabriel in the wealth of its possessions. It was famous for its fine weaving.

The church completed in 1825, the fifth church for the Santa Clara Mission, gave form to the replica built in 1929 that we see today.

After secularization, it continued as a church even though the wealth and possessions of the Mission were gone. In 1851, a need for English speaking Fathers for the new Americans, caused the Mission to be turned over to the Jesuits for a school. Four years later it became Santa Clara College, later the present university.

The church suffered a series of three fires, the last in 1926 totally destroying the building. The new church built in 1929 is the center of the University of Santa Clara campus. It also serves as a parish church and a college chapel.

Something Special

Mission Santa Clara
Santa Clara University
500 El Camino Real Box 3217
Santa Clara, CA 95053-3217
408-554-4028

Small museum at the Mission called, De Saisset Museum. There is no fund raising needed at this mission because it is supported by the University.
Activities: Daily masses are said at the mission. Weddings may be held at Mission Santa Clara. Class tours are available by special arrangement. Historical material available by sending $3 and self addressed envelope to the mission. Santa Clara University Book Store serves as a Mission book and gift store.
Hours: Self guided tours, Mon. - Fri: 8 - 6, Sun: 10:30 - Noon

Mission San Buenaventura
george kuska

San Buenaventura

(Ninth Mission, March 31, 1782)

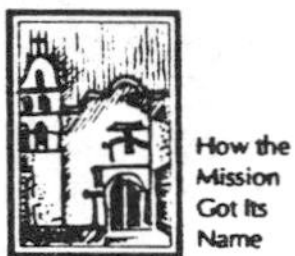

How the Mission Got Its Name

Saint Bonaventure, the patron of mission number nine, was born Giovanni de Fidanza in the hills north of Rome in 1221. According to legend, the name Bonaventure was given him by St. Francis when he healed the four year old boy and exclaimed, "O! Buena ventura!" which means "Good fortune." He became one of the great theologians and scholars of Medieval times and died at the Council of Lyons in 1274, working to unify the Eastern and Western churches.

What was to be the third Mission finally, after a 12 year delay, became the ninth Mission. It was the last Mission founded by Father Serra before his death. The long delay was caused by the discovery of San Francisco Bay that changed the priorities for settling California, and the uprising of the Yuma Indians in 1781. The Yuma revolt was against two Arizona style Missions, but it made the military in California fearful of an Indian uprising. Also, it was the result of a new government policy that made new Missions secondary to bringing Spanish settlers into Indian territory. Father Serra founded the Ventura Mission in the old style to Christianize the Indians, definitely against government policy.

The site was in a coastal area populated with about 20,000 Chumash Indians. The Chumash were among the most advanced tribes in California. They were skilled boat builders, excellent coastal seamen, fishermen, and the women knew how to weave reed baskets that were watertight.

The Mission prospered and was noted for its abundance of crops with a great variety of fruits and tropical plants. A reservoir and aqueduct system seven miles long was built to water the grain fields.

The first church burned in 1792, and was replaced in 1809 with the stone church that stands today. The large earthquake in 1812 caused much damage to the church. Almost four years of reconstruction was required to repair the building and strengthen it against future earthquakes. The large buttress at the front was added during this time.

After secularization in 1836, it served as a parish church, was sold, but was returned to the Catholic Church sixteen years later. An attempt to modernize it caused much damage to the original building. The beamed ceiling was covered over, the Indian artwork on the walls was whitewashed, and windows were enlarged and replaced with stained glass. In 1957, it was restored to its original form as much as possible. The City of Ventura has grown around the Church, but a recent plaza development in front of the building has added a sense of space for the historic structure.

Something Special

San Buenaventura Mission Museum
225 E. Main Street
Ventura, CA 93001
805-643-4318

Spanish era mission and museum.
Activities: Indian artifacts, Spanish era artifacts, and church materials.
Historic structures include 1829 adobe settling tank and 1809 church.
Literature on history of mission on sale. Permanent exhibits.
Hours: 10 - 5, Mon. - Sat: 10 - 4
Contact Msgr. Patrick J. O'Brien, Director

Mission Santa Barbara
george kuska

Santa Bárbara

(Tenth Mission, December 4, 1786)

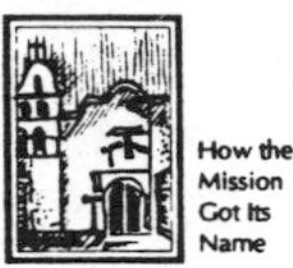
How the Mission Got Its Name

The tenth mission was named after Saint Barbara who, according to legend, was the beautiful daughter of Dioscorus of Nicomedia, a pagan Roman ruler. When Barbara became a Christian, it so angered her father that he imprisoned her and finally cut off her head with his own sword. Her father was immediately struck dead by a bolt of lightning.

Santa Bárbara, like San Diego and Monterey, was named by Sebastian Vizcaino almost 186 years before the Mission was founded. The Franciscans have had continuous control over the Mission since its founding and its record are in an unbroken sequence. This is the only California Mission which has remained so.

The presidio was founded six years before the Mission, but the Governor said it had to be this way for security reasons. Once underway, the Mission grew very fast. The Indians were Chumash, a very advanced tribe. They planted and harvested crops that ranked sixth in Mission production. They were excellent craftsmen, excelled at building and the arts, including painting and music.

The elaborate water system was a great accomplishment. The water flowed from a dam upstream from the Mission, collected in two large reservoirs, sent through filtered and settling tanks, and along elevated aqueducts to the kitchen, laundry, flour mill, and hospital, then finally to irrigate the fields and orchards. Parts of it are still used today as part of the municipal water system.

Its first permanent church, in 1789, was adobe with a tile roof. Within five years it was too small and a large church was built. It was destroyed by the earthquake in 1812. The present stone church was started shortly afterwards and dedicated in 1820. Only the left tower was completed at the time, the other being finished in 1833. It is the only Mission with twin towers.

Father Antonio Pipoll was responsible for building Mission Santa Bárbara. The Greco-Roman facade on the church was selected from a translation of Vitrivius' book on architecture written in 27 B.C. A copy was found in the Mission library.

The church continued in the hands of the Franciscans during secularization, but was damaged by a series of earthquakes. The most serious was in 1925 when one of the towers was destroyed and the second floor of the monastery severely damaged. The front of the church and towers were rebuilt to the original design in the restoration completed in 1927. Later cracks developed so, the present facade was completely rebuilt in reinforced concrete in 1950.

Mission Santa Bárbara is a true architectural gem of the Mission chain.

Something Special

Old Mission
2201 Laguna Street
Santa Barbara, CA 93001
805-682-4713

Activities: The museum store is open daily from 9 - 5. Special yearly celebrations at the mission include: The I. Madonnari Festival each Memorial Day weekend. Special activities include painting on the blacktop in front of the Old Mission. Another is, dancing on the mission steps on the first weekend of the full moon in August.

Mission La Purisima
george kuska

La Purísima Concepción

(Eleventh Mission, December 8, 1787)

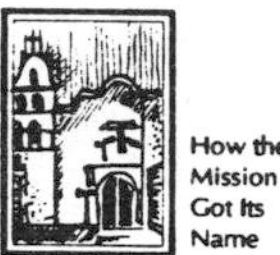

The name of the eleventh mission is "The Most Pure (Immaculate) Conception of Mary Most Holy." This is the first of two missions dedicated to Mary, the Mother of Jesus. According to doctrine, Mary was exempt from all stain of original sin and her conception of Jesus was called the Immaculate Conception.

The original site of the Mission was in the present town of Lompoc. La Purísima was favored with fertile soil and friendly Indians, but they needed to develop an elaborate irrigation system before the Mission started to prosper. By 1800, it had over 20,000 head of livestock and was third in agricultural production for all the Missions.

The first chapel and cluster of buildings were built in 1788 of wood poles and plastered with mud. In ten years this chapel was outgrown and a new church was started with adobe walls and a tile roof. This church served well a prosperous Mission until 1812.

Then catastrophe struck in the same earthquake of 1812 that damaged the large church at Santa Barbara. It leveled all the buildings of La Purísima, then broke a natural dam that flooded the ruins. Four months later, the Mission was re-established in its present location four miles north and east of its original site.

The new Mission had protection against earthquake damage with heavy buttressed stone walls. The buildings were laid out in straight lines for easier evacuation, the only Mission so arranged.

At the new site, it regained its earlier prosperity, but further disasters were to come to the Mission in its final years. It suffered a severe drought, then fire destroyed some of the buildings, and finally the Indians rebelled against the soldiers in 1824. They occupied the buildings by force and held the Mission in siege for a month. A hundred soldiers came from Monterey before the Indians surrendered to the Fathers.

After secularization, the Mission disintegrated and what few Indians remained suffered a smallpox epidemic in 1844.

The Union Oil Company finally acquired some of the land and donated it so the Mission could be restored. The National Park Service directed the work of the Civilian Conservation Corps in rebuilding it from the ground up. A trip to the restored Mission, now a State Historical Monument, is almost like visiting the Mission in its golden years.

Area Manager
Mission La Purisima Concepción
RFD # 102
Lompoc, CA 93436

State Historic Park
Activities: Mission life days with costumed (circa 1820) docents, visitors share in candle-dipping, bread making, soap making, spinning and weaving. 11 - 2.
Mid May Fiesta begins with Mass in the main church, followed by entertainment and mission-era crafts 11 - 3.
A light meal served after candlelight tours which present scenes of the past in real-life situations. (Important means of raising funds of the Prelado's many projects.)
Early December is Founding Day Celebration with musical program. Write for tickets.

Mission Santa Cruz
george kuska

Santa Cruz

(Twelfth Mission, September 25, 1791)

Holy Cross (Saint Cross) was the name given to the twelfth mission. The Cross on which Jesus Christ died is the most holy and enduring symbol of Christianity.

A very pleasant setting where the San Lorenzo River flows into Monterey Bay gave great promise to the Mission's beginning. The land was covered with lush grass and berries. Wild game was plentiful. Forests of pine and redwood covered the mountains, and the Indians were friendly. Progress was good at the new Mission, but was soon to go downhill rapidly. Santa Cruz never had more than 523 neophytes at its height.

In 1796, the Governor founded the third pueblo in California, named Branciforte, just across the river from the Mission. It was to be model city, but instead was populated with trouble makers from Mexico who founded the city rather than going to jail. The pueblo was such a degrading influence on the neophytes that over 200 left the Mission in the next two years. The Governor was petitioned to either move the pueblo or close the Mission. He decided to do neither.

Things were to get worse. Rain and high winds damaged the Mission buildings, then floods took their toll. The buildings were finally repaired to a usable condition.

In 1812, Father Andres Quintana was murdered by a group of renegade Indians in his sleep. In 1818, the rebel pirate Bouchard from Argentina was raiding the coast. He sacked Monterey. The Mission residents in Santa Cruz fled in fear that he might come in their direction. He didn't, but the people of Branciforte looted the mission worse than Bouchard and his men possibly could. Branciforte became a haven for adventurers and smugglers.

The Mission was secularized in 1834. An earthquake in 1840 destroyed the church so, by 1846, there was nothing left for Governor Pio Pico to sell. Another earthquake in 1857 tumbled the remaining walls. Mission Santa Cruz was no more.

Today a two thirds scale replica of the church stands not far from the Mission site. It was built in 1931 and generously donated to the Catholic church. Our drawing is of the replica.

Mission Santa Cruz
126 High Street
Santa Cruz, CA 95060
408-426-5686

Museum
Activities: Tours and museum visits. Call the mission for information.
Gift Shop

Mission Soledad
george kuska

Nuestra Señora de la Soledad

(Thirteenth Mission, October 9, 1791)

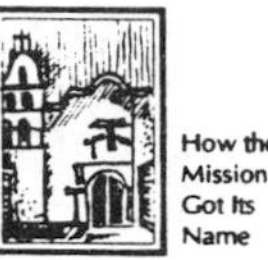
How the Mission Got Its Name

The thirteenth mission has a sad name, Our Most Sorrowful Lady of Solitude. It is the second mission named after Mary, the Mother of Jesus. The name expresses the sorrow and loneliness she feels after Jesus had been crucified.

It has been said that la Soledad "was founded in solitude and perished in neglect." The name was accidental because the natives seemed to call them selves soledad, the Spanish word for solitude. Thus the Mission was named after Our Lady of Solitude, another name for the Virgin Mary. It became a fitting name because life at the Mission was lonely and rather isolated. A total of 30 Fathers served at Soledad in the 44 years of its existence.

The lack of consistent leadership was more responsible for the Mission's reputation rather than its location. At times, the Mission managed to more than hold its own. It ranked in the middle in terms of agricultive production, which is not surprising with its location in the rich Salinas Valley. It was good cattle and sheep country in the hills. Irrigation water was available during the summer when it doesn't rain, through five miles of cemented ditch.

Several misfortunes added to Soledad's reputation. Starting in 1802, a serious epidemic killed many and drove off many more Indians. The Salinas River flooded the Mission in 1824, and even worse in 1828. The church collapsed in 1831. A store house was converted to a chapel that survived into secularization.

Father Sarria, the last Father at Soledad, kept the Mission going by himself from 1828 until he died in 1835, a year after secularization. Soledad was no longer an operating Mission.

Restoration was not started until 1954. Only one corner of wall remained intact at that time with several mounds of adobe. The chapel was built from the ground up first. More is being built as times goes on but it is still far from complete. Soledad is a parish church today. The drawing shows the rebuilt chapel.

Something Special

Old Mission
c/o Our Lady of Soledad Parish
36641 Fort Romie Road
P. O. Box 506
Soledad, CA 93960

The Mission Chapel is not a parish church.
Mass is held on Christmas Eve,
Easter Morning and on the last Sunday of June when there is a fund raiser.
On the first Sunday of October there is a wine stomp and wine auction sale.
Weddings and baptisms are permitted by appointment.

mission San Jose
george kuska

San José

(Fourteenth Mission, June 11, 1797)

Saint Joseph was chosen as the patron of our fourteenth mission. Joseph was the husband of Mary and the foster father of Jesus.

This Mission and the pueblo 15 miles south were envisioned as a base to control the Native Californians in the San Joaquin and Sacramento Valleys. Military expeditions were being sent to punish the troublesome tribes of the inland valleys, and this Mission was on the main route. The California Natives of the area were either indifferent or openly hostile to the Mission for the first few years.

However, the situation changed rapidly and San José became the most successful Mission in northern California. It ranked third behind Santa Clara and San Gabriel in the number of converts, with 6,673. It was third in livestock holdings and in total agriculture it was second only to San Gabriel.

Much of the success of the Mission is due to an extraordinary father, Narciso Duran, who supervised it for 27 years. He excelled at everything he tried. He directed the elaborate Mission enterprises, planned military strategy against hostile California Natives, constructed irrigation systems, and not the least of all, he wrote and taught music. His Native American orchestra became famous and played European instruments.

The Mission suffered the usual decline after secularization, but remained in use as a parish church. Slow deterioration was taking effect when the October 12, 1868 earthquake on the Hayward Fault brought the Mission to a violent end. The quake was considered the strongest in the recorded history of California. Only a small fragment of the West Wing of the quadrangle that once covered five acres remained of the mission period and it was restored in 1916.

Original stone foundations were found during archaelolgical excavations. Starting in 1982, a replica of the mission chapel of about 1835 has been built on these original foundations. Our drawing on the opposite page is of this replica.

Old Mission San Jose Museum
43300 Mission Boulevard
P. O. Box 3159
Fremont, CA 94539
510-657-1797

Historic park.
Admission receipts go toward the Mission Restoration Fund.
Activities: An 1810 adobe residence and authentically reconstructed church with collections related to the Spanish mission era and Native Americans (the Ohlone).
Mission Days held each year on the weekend closest to June 11.
Las Posadas are held each year for the nine evenings before Christmas.
Docent tours for groups of 20 or more are available by arrangement.
Contact: Kerey Ty Quaid, Curator

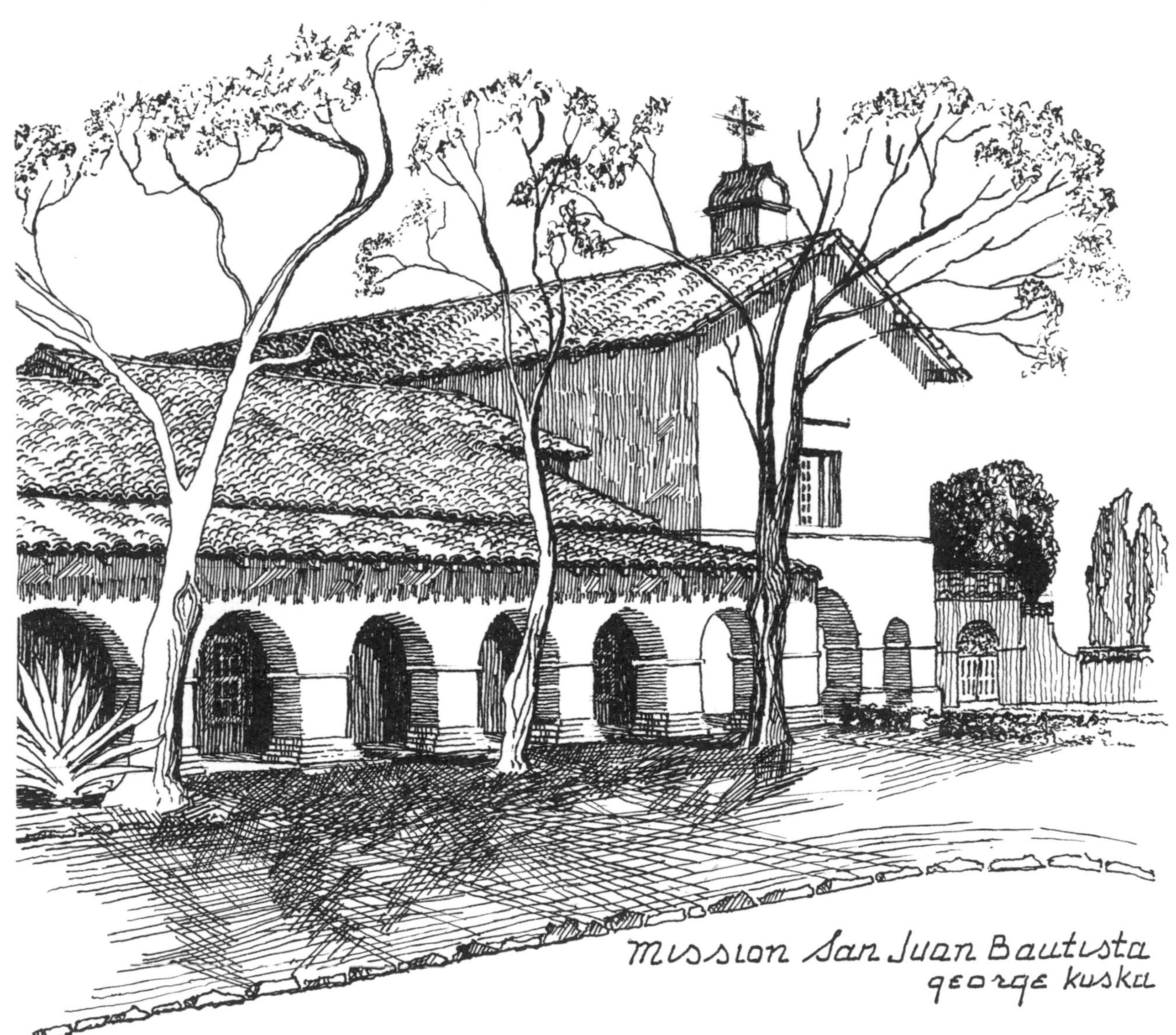
Mission San Juan Bautista
george kuska

San Juan Bautista

(Fifteenth Mission, June 24, 1797)

How the Mission Got Its Name

The fifteenth mission is named in honor of Saint John the Baptist. John the Baptist was a forerunner of Jesus and the person who baptised him.

The Mission lies in a gentle, sunny valley separated from the Salinas Valley by the Gabilan Mountains. It has been a parish church continuously since its founding, and its setting has changed little from a hundred years ago.

From the very beginning, it drew a large number of converts. Within six months they had constructed the Mission complex. By 1800, there were over 500 Native Californians living at the Mission. An earthquake caused considerable damage in October of that year. In rebuilding it, the Fathers enlarged the church. Even so, by 1803, a new larger church was started; the one that is there today. Father Arroyo de la Cuesta wanted a church for 1,000 worshipers without the long, narrow nave. He convinced the builders that it should have a side aisle on each side of the nave, or basically a church with three naves side by side. When the building was finished in 1812, it was the largest and the only one of its kind.

By the time the church was finished, the Native American population was reduced to half through death and desertion. The church was too large so Cuesta walled in the two rows of arches that separated the naves thus forming a church with one nave.

For most of its existence, the Mission was guided by Father Cuesta and Father Tapis, two most remarkable Fathers. Father Cuesta had a gift for language, as well as being architect, scholar, and musician.

He mastered seven Native American dialects, could give his sermons in their own tongue, and could communicate with his charges in their language. Father Tapis was an accomplished musician and had a special talent for music. He used colored notes to identify the different vocal parts so the Native Americans could read music in choral singing.

The Mission had a flourishing trade with Yankee ships at Monterey, trading hides and tallow, mostly for machinery.

After secularization in 1834, the Native Americans gradually left, but the church was never without a priest.

A wooden steeple was added by Father Rubio in 1867. The steeple was damaged by a wind storm in 1915. The design was changed to a shorter version only to be modified again to a more mission style stucco bell tower. That was finally removed in 1949.

In 1976, extensive reconstruction and restoration returned the Mission to its original three naves. Once again, it is California's largest mission church. A new bell wall (campanario) was added where stone foundations were found to indicate one may have been originally intended. The design is similar to the one at San Diego, but it is a completely new addition where one had never before existed.

The passing of time has enriched rather than destroyed this mission. To appreciate mission architecture and a feeling of the mission period, in the authentic setting of San Juan Bautista, there is an experience to be savored and enjoyed.

Something Special

Mission San Juan Bautista
2nd and Mariposa Streets
P. O. Box 410
San Juan Bautista, CA 95045
408-623-2127

Museum and Spanish mission.
Activities: Collection in mission rooms relating to history of the mission, founded in 1797. Guided tours. Museum related items for sale. Various publications.
Hours: Mar-Oct: 9-5, daily; Nov-Feb, 9:30-4:30; tours by appointment
Contact: Rev. Max Santamaria

Mission San Miguel
George Kuska

San Miguel Arcángel

(Sixteenth Mission, July 25, 1797)

How the Mission Got Its Name

The sixteenth mission is named after Saint Michael, the leader of God's Army against Satan. He is considered the chief of the archangels and the protector of Christians, particularly at the hour of death.

Presidente Fermin de Lasuén founded four missions in four months. San Miguel was the third, located halfway between San Luis Obispo and San Antonio de Padua. The start of the mission was very encouraging. A large crowd of Native Americans gathered for the dedication ceremonies. Fifteen children were baptized that day. In less than ten years there were nearly a thousand Native American people at the mission. However, there was a specific understanding that every effort would be made to attract the Tulare Indians from the San Joaquin valley. They were warlike tribes who resented any intrusion of the white man. Historical records indicate the Mission had very little success in this ambitious program.

The Mission was located in a fertile valley near the meeting place of the Nacimiento and Salinas rivers. It quickly developed and became a thriving community.

In 1806, a serious fire destroyed a number of buildings and part of the church roof. The most immediate damage was to the stores of wool, cloth, leather goods and over 6,000 bushels of grain. With help from the other Missions, San Miguel soon recovered.

Work on the new church was started in 1816. The Native California workers had begun making adobe bricks, floor tile, and roof tile for the new church almost ten years earlier. They then cut and hauled 44 foot long roof timbers from pine forests 25 miles away. The walls were finished in two years because of the previous years of work, but the roof took an additional year to complete. Five years later, artist Esteban Munras taught and directed the Native Americans in fresco work that gives the interior a special radiance that is still there today.

The arcade in front of the priest's quarters is unique. The flowing rhythm of a series of arches found in all the other missions is here syncopated by differences in width, height, and shape. To the casual observer, it appears chaotic, but a definite pattern exists. The first arch at each end is smaller and semicircular, followed by four larger ones, then a large elliptical arch on each side of the center. The imagination of this design has not been explained, nor was it duplicated in any of the other missions.

The 2,000 pound mission bell is the largest bell in any of the missions. It was cast in 1888 using bells sent to San Miguel from the other missions. It rang for the first time on Christmas Day, 1888. Father Jose Mut was the priest at the time, and is the only priest buried in the Mission San Miguel Cemetery.

San Miguel was one of the last missions secularized. The last Franciscan left in 1841. The property was sold and parts of the priest's quarters were used as a series of stores. In 1859 the property was returned to the Catholic Church. The church was unattended for long periods of time and it is surprising that the interior remains in its original condition. In 1928 the mission was returned to the Franciscans. Today it is a parish church and is maintained in a manner to express its rich history.

Something Special

Mission San Miguel
Mission Street
P. O. Box 69
San Miguel, CA 93451
805-467-3256

Spanish era mission.
Activities: Artifacts of old mission days, original rooms, murals, and paintings.
A Mission Fiesta is held yearly in September.
Self guided tours.
Hours: 10 - 5, daily
Contact: Rev. Clifford Herle, O. F. M., Director

Mission San Fern ndo Rey de España
george kuska

San Fernando Rey de España

(Seventeenth Mission, September 8, 1797)

Ferdinand, King of Spain, after whom the seventeenth mission was named, was born near Salamanca in 1198. He became King Ferdinand III of Castille when he was eighteen years old and King of Leon, thirteen years later. He was successful in driving the Moors out of most of Spain and proved to be a very good ruler. He died in 1252.

San Fernando was the fourth Mission founded by Father Lasuen in a four months period in 1797. They were all part of the inland chain of Missions located to maintain a day's travel distance between Missions. As with the other inland Missions, success was almost immediate. Many Indians attended the dedication and ten children were baptised that day. Within two months a small church was completed and forty neophytes were living at the Mission.

The founding of the Mission was different in several respects. The site for the buildings was on a private rancho owned by Don Francisco Reyes, a Spanish settler. There seems to be some question whether he received the land as a grant from the King or just settled on it. But he obviously gave it up gracefully for the Mission.

The Mission then was less than a day's travel from the well established and rapidly growing peublo of Los Angeles. The Mission became the most popular place to stop for travelers from Los Angeles on El Camino Real. Overnight guests were always welcome at the Mission. The need for hospice space resulted in construction of the famous "long building." After thirteen years it was to reach 243 feet in length. It is today the largest original structure remaining in the Mission chain and the largest adobe building in California. The long two-story building proved valuable to subsequent owners after secularization. It remained intact and well maintained. The church wasn't so lucky. The roof tiles were sold and the walls allowed to erode away.

Gold was discovered on an outer rancho of the Mission in 1843, five years before the great California gold discovery. A mini-rush occurred after this discovery, but the scale of the gold find did not excite too many people.

San Fernando was involved in military operations on several occasions. It was the military headquarters for California governors from 1833 until 1846, and John C. Fremont made it his headquarters after he captured it in 1847.

In 1896, The Landmark Club started a campaign to restore the buildings. Restoration has been more or less continuous ever since. The earthquake of 1971 caused considerable damage.

San Fernando Mission and Historical Museum/ Archival Center
15151 San Fernando Mission Boulevard
Mission Hills, CA 91345
818-361-0186 or 365-1501 for museum

Archives and/or manuscript repository and a mission complex and museum
Activities: Mission founded in 1797. Collections related to the mission and its buildings. Docent programs, tours. Publications include quarterly newsletter, *Friends of Archival Center* and brochures and pamphlet.
Hours: Mission: 9 - 4:30, Mon - Fri
Contact: Msgr. Francis J. Weber, Director and Archivist

Mission San Luis Rey
george kuska

San Luís Rey de Francia

(Eighteenth Mission, June 13, 1798)

Louis IX, King of France, was the namesake of the eighteenth mission. He was born in 1215, and became king at the age of eleven when his father died. He was the leader of two crusades. The first one was to Egypt in 1248 in which he was taken captive. The second crusade was to Tunis in 1270 where he died of typhus.

The timing was ideal for the founding of this Mission. Although a very late Mission, it became one of the most successful. The Indians were almost anxious to become part of this new enterprise, and could see the definite economic advantages in their lives.

One of the important reasons for the success or failure of any Mission was the Father-in-charge. For San Luís Rey, this talented man was Father Antonio Peyri who directed its fortunes from the founding for the next thirty-three years. The organizing genius of Father Peyri developed an endless number of thriving industries. The extent of its land holdings, the size of its herds of sheep, cattle, and horses, and even the size of the Indian village was greater than that of any other Mission.

Father Peyri proved to be an able architect as well. He drew the plans and supervised construction of a vast array of buildings and other construction projects such as an intricate aqueduct system, large open-air laundry and bath facilities with pools of charcoal-filtered water, and extensive gardens.

The large church that exists today was started in 1811 and finished in 1815 — remarkable in itself when we realize the great stone church at San Juan Capistrano was destroyed by an earthquake in 1812. The church is the most sophisticated architecturally and one of the most interesting of all the Missions. The plan is in the form of a cross (cruciform) similar to the ruined church at San Juan Capistrano, the only other so constructed. It has an elaborate octagonal baptistry roofed with a dome, and another dome over the cross. Later a raised lantern with windows for light was built on top of this dome. The title "King of the Missions" is in part due to the church construction.

Father Peyri left the Mission in 1832 because of pressure from the new Mexican government and the approach of secularization. What was left was sold in 1846. President Lincoln signed the decree returning the Missions to the church in 1861, but by then the desolation was almost complete.

Franciscan Fathers from Mexico asked for and received permission to establish a seminary in 1893 at the Mission. Restoration continued off and on from then until 1950 when it was substantially complete. The church remains now very much as it was during its glory days.

Mission San Luís Rey Museum
4050 Mission Avenue
San Luis Rey, CA 93068
619-757-4613

Historic mission and museum.
Activities: Native American baskets, Spanish period artifacts, ecclesiastical furnishings.
Tours to groups by appointment.
Hours: 10 - 4, Mon - Sat: 12 - 4, Sun
Contact: Mary C. Whelan, Director

Mission Santa Ines
george kuska

Santa Inés

(Nineteenth Mission, September 17, 1804)

How the Mission Got Its Name

The nineteenth mission was named after Saint Agnes. She was a thirteen year old Roman girl killed for believing in Christ. This was in 304 A. D. during the persecutions of the Christians by the Emperor Diocletian.

The last of the southern Missions and nineteenth over all, was founded by Father Estevan Topis to serve the numerous Indians inland, across the mountains from Santa Barbara. The Indians were aware of the missionary effort so over 200 were present when the blessing was bestowed. Twenty children were baptized.

Santa Ines had all of the possibilities of becoming an outstanding Mission. Even though it was moderately successful, it never lived up to its great potential. Its pleasant setting in the beautiful valley of the Santa Ines River gave no indication of the troubles that would keep it from that potential.

The strong earthquake of 1812 destroyed many of the numerous building constructed at the Mission and damaged the church to the extent that five years of reconstruction were required before it was rededicated. During that time a new long building was hastily built to be used as a church, then later used as a granary when it was no longer needed for religious services.

Starting in 1810, the Missions had to support the military forces stationed to guard them. After Mexico gained her independence in 1821, the cost to support the soldiers was increased. Indians resented doing so much for the idle soldiers and taking abuse from them also. In 1824, after a soldier beat a neophyte for a minor infraction, open revolt resulted in an attack by the Indians on the Mission. They burned some of the buildings, but when the church started to burn, the Indians paused long enough to help put the fire out. Even though the revolt was not against the Fathers, Indian relations were never the same again.

In 1836, Santa Inés was shared with the civil administration, a first step to secularization. The decline was rapid but the Mission was saved from complete ruin by an agreement between the Governor and the Bishop to open a college. Opened in 1844, it became the first college in California. The College of Our Lady of Refuge. It was later moved and remained open only until 1881.

The first real effort to restore the Mission was in 1904 by the parish priest, Father Alexander Buckler. In 1924, the Capuchin Franciscans took over. Major reconstruction work was done in 1947 and 1953.

Something Special

Old Mission Santa Ines
1760 Mission Drive
P. O. Box 408
Solvang, CA 93463
805-688-4815

Spanish era mission.
Activities: Mexican and Spanish art and tools, vestments, and archaeological sites.
Museum related items for sale.
Hours: Winter: 9:30 - 4:30, Mon - Sat, and 12 - 4:30, Sun;
Summer: 9:30 - 5:30, Mon - Sat, and 12 - 5, Sun
Contact: Shirley Rowley, Director

Mission San Rafael Arcángel
george kuska

San Rafael Arcángel

(Twentieth Mission, December 14, 1817)

How the Mission Got Its Name

Saint Raphael, one of the three archangels named in the Bible, was the patron saint of the twentieth mission. His name means "God heals." He is the patron saint of travelers, of joy, and against illness.

San Rafael Mission was founded as a branch of Mission Dolores for one primary reason, and a secondary reason acceptable to the civil authorities. The weather at Mission Dolores, especially in the summer, was damp, foggy and cold. The Native Americans were not able to tolerate this climate. Hundreds had died, and many more were chronically ill. Just north across the bay, San Rafael was protected by the mountain from the wind and fog, offering a warmer, dry climate for the sick neophytes. It was founded as a sanitarium for the sick from Mission Dolores, and named after the Archangel Raphael.

The secondary reason was the Russians, who had established a fur trading outpost at Ft. Ross in 1812. The Spanish didn't want them to expand further south into this territory.

Father Luis Gil y Toboado from La Purísima Mission was asked to be an advisor on establishing the sanitarium, being the only Father in California with some medical training. Father Gil volunteered to run the Mission branch, with immediate success. Before long, the sick from other Missions were also being sent to San Rafael. It not only was a healing place for the sick, but the Mission prospered and became self-sufficient.

The buildings were not complicated or imposing. They consisted of a church with a long wing for the Father's quarters, workshops, storerooms, and hospital wards. It is supposed the church had a star window like, but smaller than Carmel, as its only decoration. Even this is not known for certain. It was raised to the status of a full Mission in 1823.

San Rafael was the first Mission secularized. General Vallejo took over the lands and livestock to protect them from improper use, and for later distribution to the Native Americans. Vallejo had much land as a probable result of this. The Mission was abandoned in 1855. By 1861 the building was sold to a carpenter who demolished the remains to salvage the handhewn beams.

In 1949 a replica of the Mission was built with a donation from the Hearst Foundation. The replica faces the mountains, the original faced the bay. This drawing is of the replica.

Something Special

Mission San Rafael
1104 5th Street
San Rafael, CA 94901
415-456-3016

The Mission San Rafael Gift Shop is open seven days a week from 11 to 4. Mission artifacts are on display.

Mission San Francisco Solano
george kuska

San Francisco de Solano

(Twenty-first Mission, July 4, 1823)

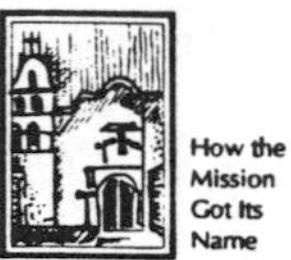
How the Mission Got Its Name

The twenty-first and last mission founded in Alta California was named in honor of Saint Francis Solanus. Francis Solanus was born in Montilla, Spain in 1549 of noble parents. He became a Franciscan missionary to South America. He had remarkable skill with languages and could quickly learn to talk to the Native Americans in their own language.

Still fearful that the Russians might move farther south, the Spanish authorities planned a series of settlements to extend north almost to Ft. Ross. Missions were to be established at Sonoma, Santa Rosa, and Napa with a presidio at Bodega Bay.

Into this plan came a young Father stationed at Mission Dolores, Father Jose Altimira. Recently arrived in California from Spain, Father Altimira was full of missionary zeal and anxious to convert the Indians. He developed an ambitious scheme to close the Missions at Dolores and San Rafael, with the idea of combining all of their assets into one large, prosperous Mission farther north. Without the knowledge or approval of Father President Senan, Father Altimira received approval from the Governor and founded the Mission at Sonoma. When the Church authorities learned of the scheme, they rebuked both the Governor and Father Altimira. A compromise was finally reached to let the Mission at Sonoma remain as San Francisco Solano, but Mission Dolores and San Rafael would also continue.

Father Altimira lacked leadership abilities and in about two years, the Indians revolted against his harsh treatment and forced him to flee to San Rafael.

A large adobe church was completed in 1833, but by then the winds of change were too much to allow development as a typical Mission. General Vallejo took over the Mission after secularization as chief administrator in 1835.

Vallejo is responsible for building the present chapel in 1840 because decay of the large church was so rapid.

The Russians withdrew from Ft. Ross in 1841. The increasing number of Americans were afraid Mexico wanted them out of California, so on June 14, 1846 some of the Americans took over Sonoma and made Vallejo a prisoner. They flew a crude flag with a grizzly bear and star, declaring California an independent republic. The republic lasted 23 days before Commodore Sloat raised the American flag in Monterey.

Vallejo's chapel that stands today has been restored a number of times. The Landmarks League in 1903 bought the ruins, but the 1906 earthquake damaged the remains so work was very slow. The state acquired the building in 1926, restored it again in 1944, and it is now a State Historical Monument.

Something Special

Sonoma State Historic Park
20 East Spain Street
Sonoma, CA 95476
707-938-2588

California State Historic Park and house museum.
Activities: Sonoma (Mexican) Barracks (1846), San Francisco Solano de Sonoma Mission (1823), Toscano Hotel (1852), and Vallejo Home (1852).
Hours: 10 - 5 daily
Contact: Larry Ferri

View Spanish California Today

Often parents and/or community members will be a big help in sharing experiences, craft pieces, recipes, to say nothing of themselves.

Walking field trips to Mexican stores of all kinds; supermercados will be a big help.

If you take a Mission trip, plan what to look for with the children.

There is hardly a book on Missions that doesn't have at least one artifact pictured which can be shown through opaque or overhead projectors.

Be sure to check your Instructional Media Center for more films, film strips, slides, and other resources they may have.

Remember that the ultimate goal here is to help build for boys and girls understandings to their fullest of the California Missions, as a part of history, and as they influence our lives today.

Environmental Board

1. Arrange children in groups of five or six. Each group will have one board *(cardboard or wood, about the size of two desk tops)*
2. Using any materials available to them and appropriate to the task, children will build an environment representing a piece of California land. It may be two or three dimensional. Teacher should begin by listing some elements that all boards should have, such as:
   - a water source
   - a wooded area
   - a grassy area
   - hills

   Let them represent this in any way they choose. They could use paint, colored paper, clay, pipe cleaners, materials some kids have for building model train outfits. Some may want to include animal figures *(this should be okay if historically and geographically accurate – deer, yes, tigers no.).*
3. Prepare ditto to be duplicated on tagboard, with small drawn figures of people, such as missionaries, soldiers, settlers, and Indians. You might wish to make two dittos with the first, Indians, then settlers.
4. After preparation of "environment" give each group a card of people. Let them cut the figures apart and then show answers to specific questions. *For Indians, it might be . . . .* How would they provide shelter? How would they find food in this area? How would they protect themselves from dangers? *For settlers, it might be . . . .* How would a group of missionaries use this area? Where would they build houses? Where would they grow crops? Where could settlements be built for trading? Later, for both groups, questions, such as: How would Indians and settlers live together in this area?

As learning goes on, models of Missions or of settlements could be added to the boards.

How Hides Were Prepared for Shipment

The hide of the cattle was probably the most important part of the animal to the ranchero. The hides were used for many things in early California. Hides and also tallow were used almost like money in trading on the ships that came, bringing clothes and many other fine things desired by the people of California.

When the hide was taken from the animal it was spread out and staked to dry. They were then put through a process called curing. This made them easier to handle and helped to keep them from spoiling. They were soaked in a very salty water solution for many hours and then spread out to dry. They were then stretched on the ground and were left to dry. Next they were powdered with salt. When the hides were ready, men folded them in half with the hair on the outside.

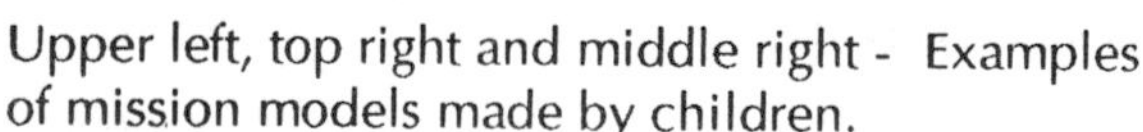

Upper left, top right and middle right - Examples of mission models made by children.

Bottom right - Mural depicting making adobe bricks.

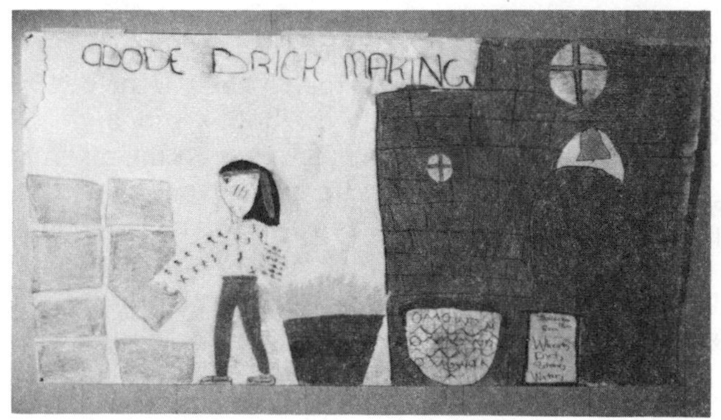

Getting in Touch

Instead of having pen pals really far away, find a new friend or a class in California with whom to correspond. If you live near a Mission, find a class in the mountains or in the desert; if you live far away from the Missions you might want to find some children near a Mission. This will broaden the the scope of understanding of the state. Share the Spanish names of places with your pen class. What questions might you ask?

Teachers and parents: Check state school directories for public or private school addresses.

From CSAA get maps and hunt for Spanish names.

Dear Mom, Dad, Boys, Girls, and Teachers:

At some time during the fourth grade you will probably want to write to a Mission. Check the address and status of your special Mission and enclose a stamped, self-addressed envelope for easy answering.

Wire Weaving with Bobby Pin Shuttle

Use a wire cutter, cut chicken wire or hardware cloth into the desired shape. Cover all the cut ends of the wire with masking tape. Weave designs and patterns on the wire with yarn, ribbon, and string of all sorts of colors, textures, and thicknesses. Tie one end of the material to the wire. Pierce the other end with a bobby pin and pull it through to the closed end of the pin. Weave over and under the wires – one, two, three, or more at a time. When you are finished with any one kind of material, tie to the wire frame. Then tie the new piece to the frame, poke in the bobby pin, and continue weaving. The protective masking tape can be removed, or replaced with cloth tape, when the piece is finished. You'll get a true weaving feeling and can make your own Mission Indian hanging or table mats. Try dyeing your own yarns with vegetable dyes.

Papier Maché Made Easy

The easiest way of making papier maché objects is to apply glued strips of newspapers, paper towels, craft paper – whatever paper you have on hand – to a base. Strips that have been torn rather than cut have a rough edge and will mesh together for a smoother surface. If you are applying several layers of strips, it is wise to use a different color or type of of paper for each layer. You can alternate between white and colored newspaper or paper toweling, using white facial tissue for the final cover. Use mash for giving texture.

Bases that can be used:

- boxes for Mission making
- tuna cans with paper cylinders for candle holders
- t.v. dinner trays can be molded for masks

Paper Mash. Paper mash, or pulp, is made by soaking or cooking paper in water and combining with starch to form a malleable substance. It can be molded over a base, or by itself, and used to add texture or to build up specific areas. There are several commercial mixes available for making "instant" paper mash. These mixtures are easy to work with and readily available at hobby or craft stores also.

Sheet Papier-Maché. Stack two sheets of white paper towel or facial tissue on top of four sheets of newspaper. Draw the shape you want on the top sheet in crayon or pencil. Cut this shape out of the stack of papers. Brush or sponge a heavy coat of liquid starch over each layer of the cut-out shape. Press the layers together firmly. Sculpture by bending, pleating, or folding. Large pieces must be put over a box, can, or bottle to hold the shape while drying. Let sculpture dry for 24 to 36 hours.

Book Binding

Punch three matching holes in the pages and in the front and back covers of the book. With a straight edge or rule, fold and crease the front cover about two inches from its left end to make a hinge. Stack the pages and covers together so that the holes align. Thread the holes with ribbon, yarn, or string and tie the book together.

Mission Music

Music was a part of Mission life. Both the Indian groups and the Spanish had used chants and singing for work, worship and pleasure. The Mission Bells were important, and pealed far and wide to bring workers out of the fields to meal or worship.

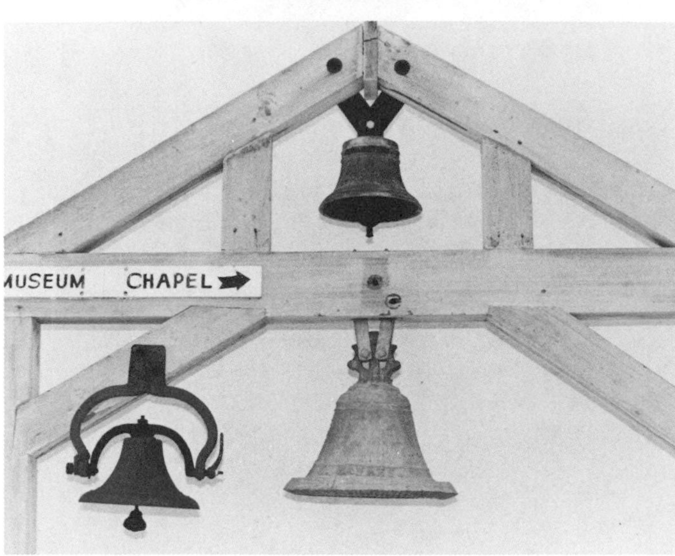

MUSIC & RHYTHM

Simple rhythm instruments are made and used to give a beat to renditions.

Matracas are grooved implements that are rubbed together to make a grating sound.

Maracas are made for shaking. Small pebbles or seeds in an enclosed box or gourd will make an effective sound if done in systematic rhythm.

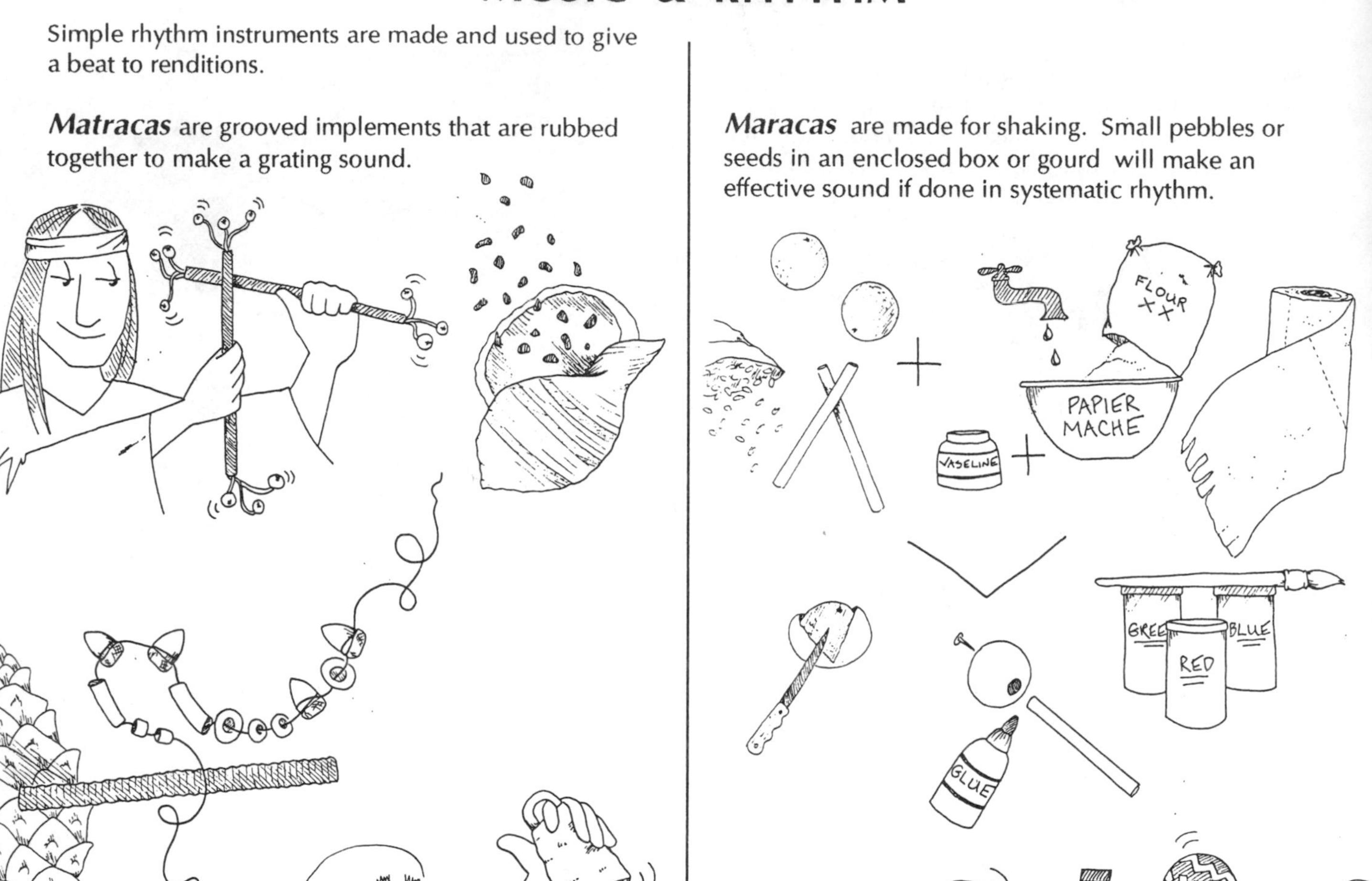

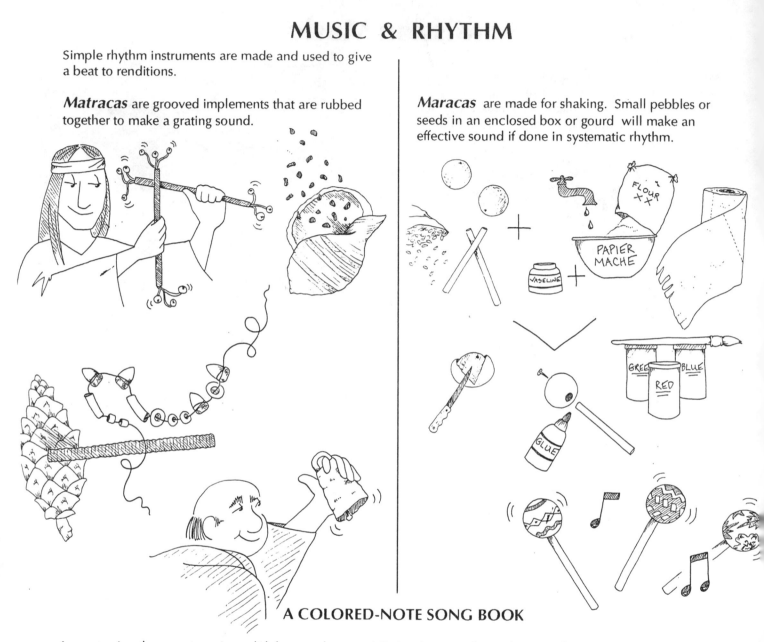

A COLORED-NOTE SONG BOOK

Learn to sing three part music as did the neophytes at Mission Santa Barbara. (See article on Page 93)
We can write chants telling of many things that went on at the Missions. With an easy-to-use sample of a simple, but significant poem, try the following with ***red** (higher voices)* ***blue** (lower voices) etc.*:

red	SO	LA	SO	SO	SO	SO
yellow	MI	FA	MI	MI	RE	MI
blue	DO	DO	DO	DO	TI	DO
	Get	*up*	*now,*	*tend*	*the*	*plow*

red	SO	SO	SO	SO	LA	SO
yellow	MI	RE	MI	MI	FA	MI
blue	DO	TI	DO	DO	DO	DO
	Horse	*in*	*hand,*	*round*	*the*	*bend*

red	SO	SO	LA	SO	LA	SO
yellow	MI	RE	MI	MI	FA	MI
blue	DO	DO	DO	DO	DO	DO
	Morn -	*ing*	*light,*	*birds*	*in*	*flight*

red	SO	SO	LA	SO	SO	SO
yellow	MI	MI	FA	RE	RE	MI
blue	DO	DO	DO	TI	TI	DO
	Time	*to*	*dine,*	*get*	*in*	*line.*

Mission Life Word Search

You will find among these letters 30 words related to people and things about the Missions.

The words are found by reading up, down, forward, backward and even diagonally. Enclose each word by drawing lines around it.

Parents and teachers: challenge yourselves and your youngsters by hiding the key for a spell.

acorn	bellows	corn	game	olla	San Diego
adobe	brick	dance	hides	Pacific	Serra
baja	burro	el camino	horses	padre	Solano
baskets	caballo	farm	Indian	pomo	tallow
bell	carreta	fiesta	Mission	roots	vaca

This puzzle was created by "Aunt" Margaret Johnson.

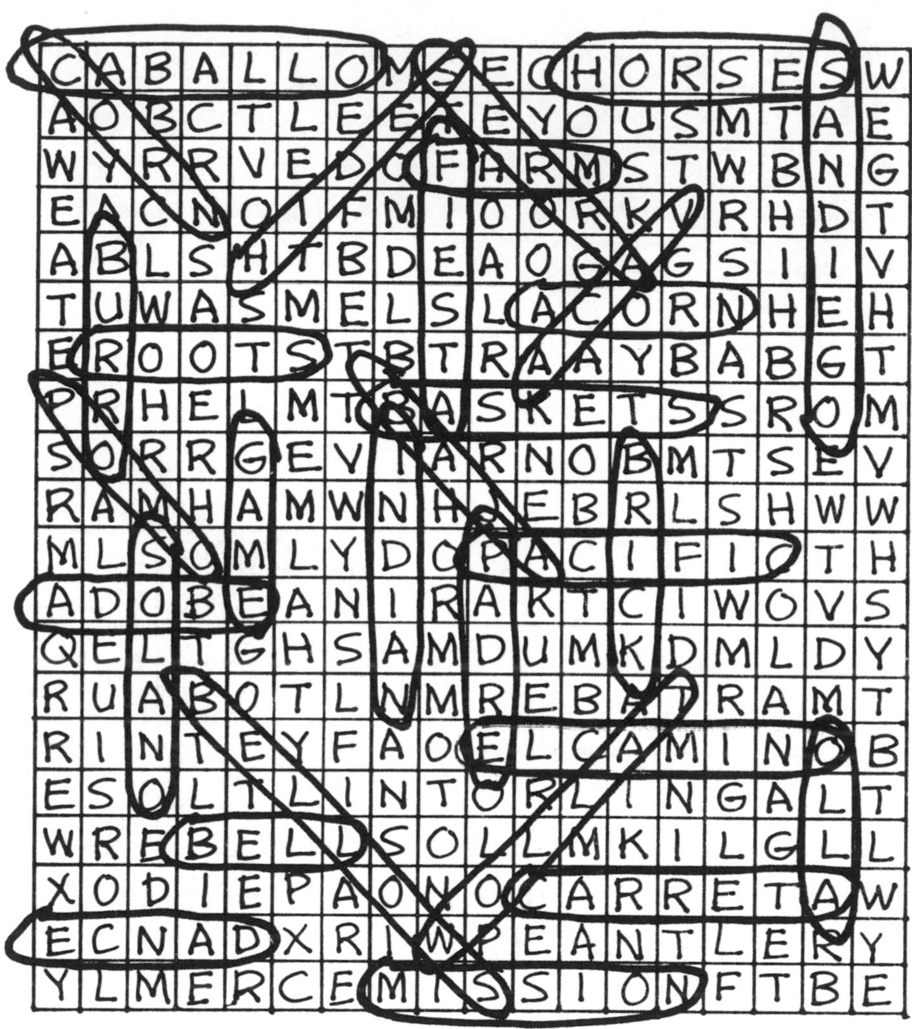

HERE IS THE SOLUTION! HOW DID YOU DO?

Mission Crafts and Skills

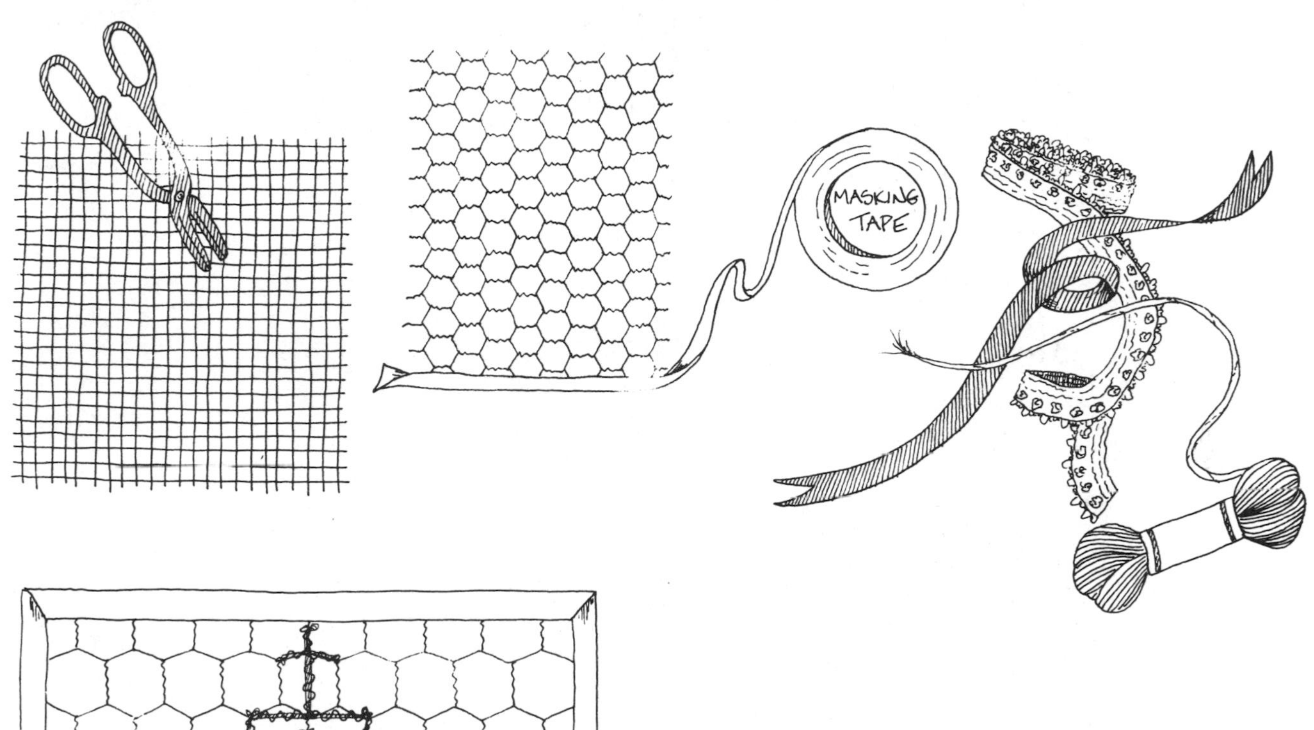

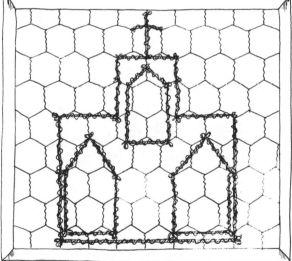

MISSION WEAVING

Large looms were used for cloth making in increasing numbers throughout the years. To give the feeling of weaving a pattern use chicken wire or hardware cloth is suggested as step 1. Box looms, waist looms, and card looms are among other simple homemade looms you might want to use in your home or classroom.

Materials – Wire
– Yarn
– Safety pins
– Bobby pins

MISSION MODELS have been made of everything from graham crackers to carved styrafoam *(carved gently with a sharp knife).* Little adobe bricks are certainly the most authentic. Corrugated cardboard and lasagne noodles are among the materials which can be used to make ripply roofs.

Materials – See the choices.

MISSION WALL FRIEZE OR DECORATION

Many of the Missions had simple patterns painted on the walls.

Many of the Missions had geometric or natural patterns painted on their walls.

How to Do It

Create a dozen zig zags and California poppies or oak leaves and acorns by repeating the patterns over and over with tempera and a brush on manila paper, a wall or shelf paper. Make geometric designs with starch and tempera and applying with fingers on shelf or butcher paper.

Materials — Hands or brushes.
— Shelf paper
— Paint and starch to equal finger paint

PLANT A MISSION GARDEN

Check your list of Mission produce for authenticity. If you haven't space outside, flower pots inside are fine.

WIRE COAT HANGER BRANDS

What are brands? With the coming of cattle to California and the separation into herds came the need to distinguish between different owners. Pieces of iron were forged into shapes peculiar to each ranch and Mission. This method of identification is used today. The iron is put in hot coals then onto the steer's flank.

Make your own shape or copy some you find here or in a library Mission or rancho book. Unwind the coat hanger; bend it into shape; and hang it up. Don't dump it in the coals!

Materials — Wire hanger

JOURNAL LOG AND DIARY KEEPING are useful experiences. The content can come from reading, from movies, individual projects or can be your own imagination of what some of these early experiences might have been.

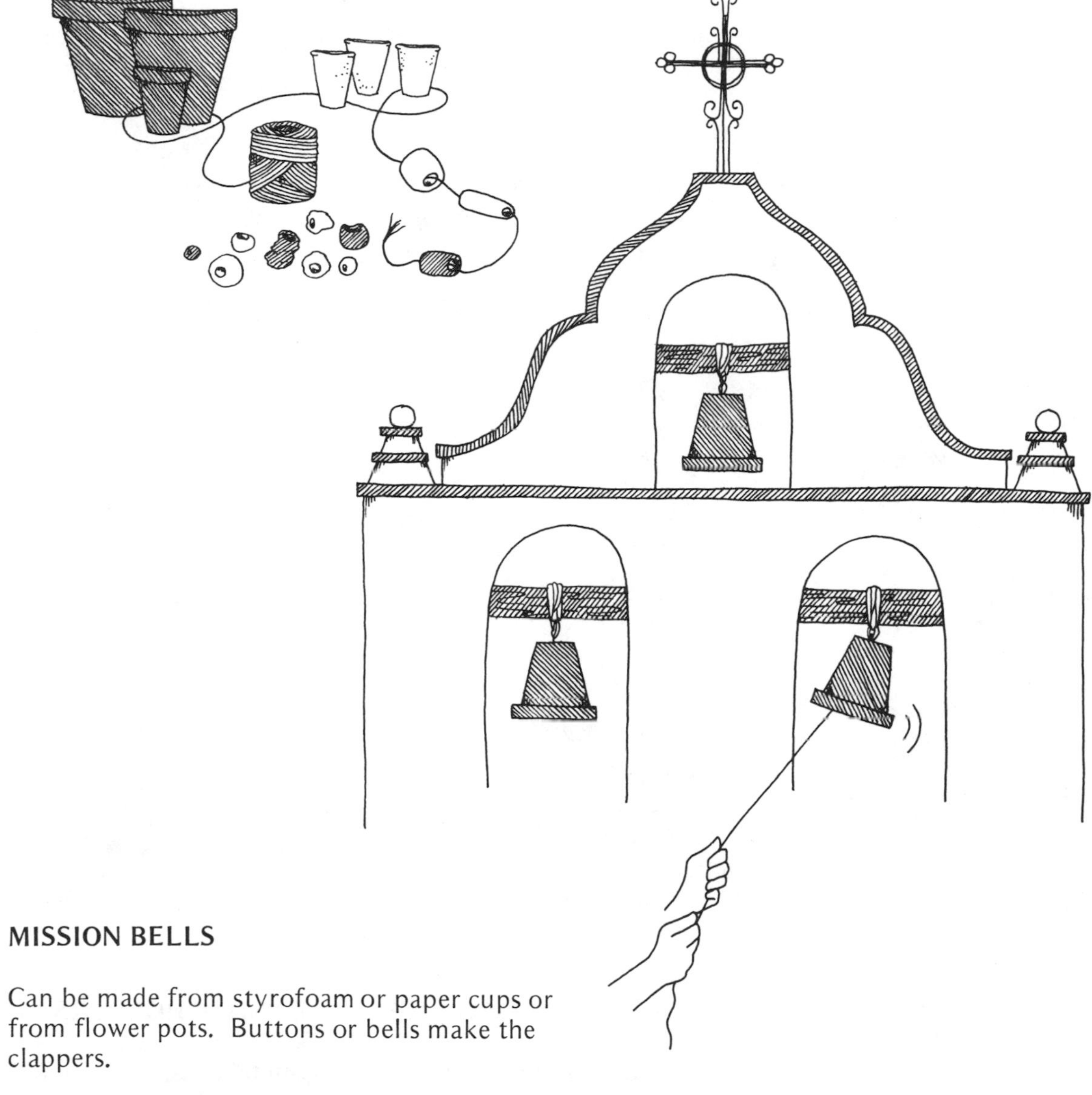

MISSION BELLS

Can be made from styrofoam or paper cups or from flower pots. Buttons or bells make the clappers.

Materials — Flower pots
— Seeds or bells
— Cups
— String

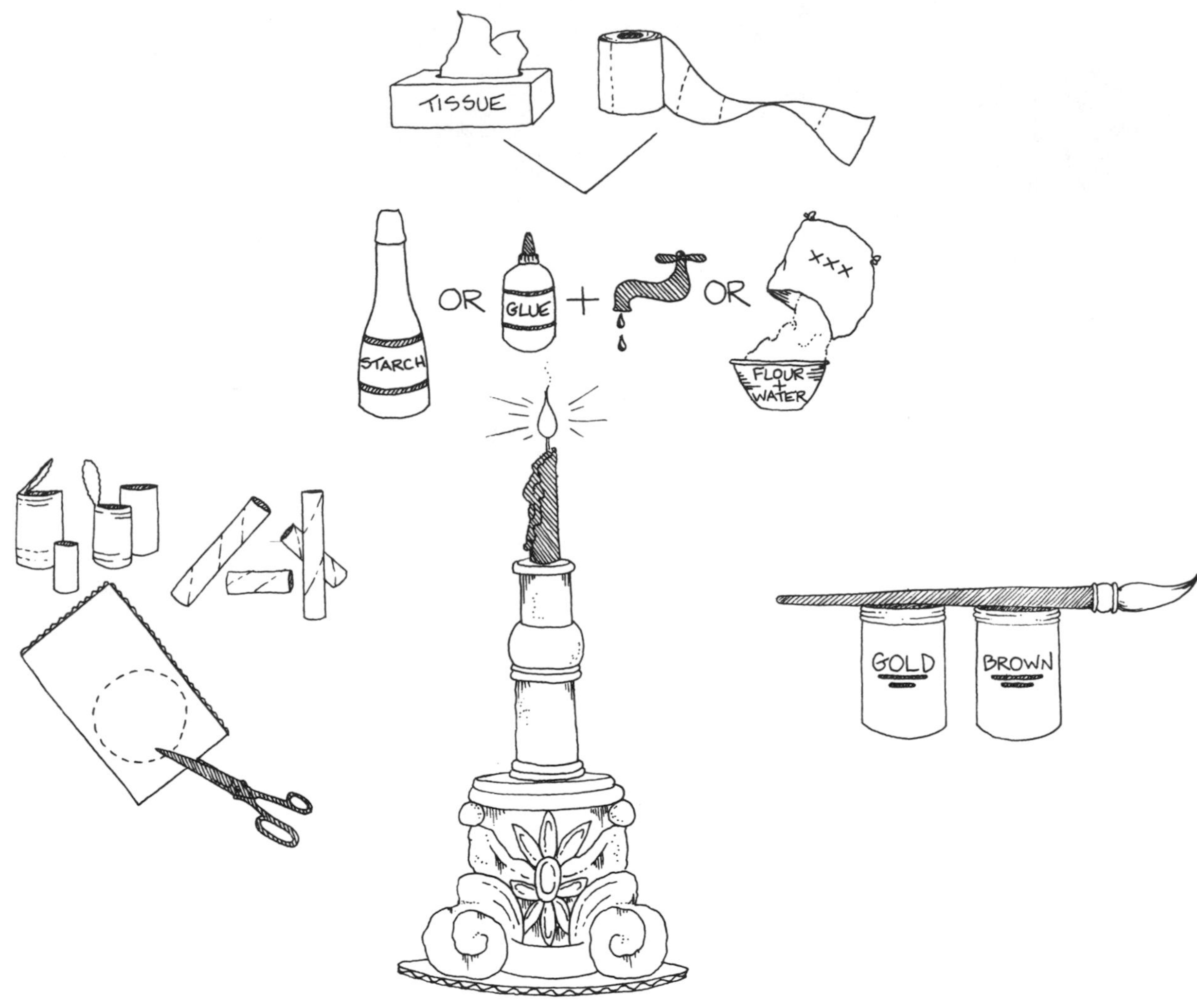

PAPIER MACHÉ MISSION CANDLE HOLDERS

Use cardboard circles, tubes, metal cans, spools and papier maché from toilet tissue and flour and water paste. Apply and mold with hands or sticks. Dry and paint.

Materials — Cardboard - flat or cylinders
— Scissors
— Mache
— Paint

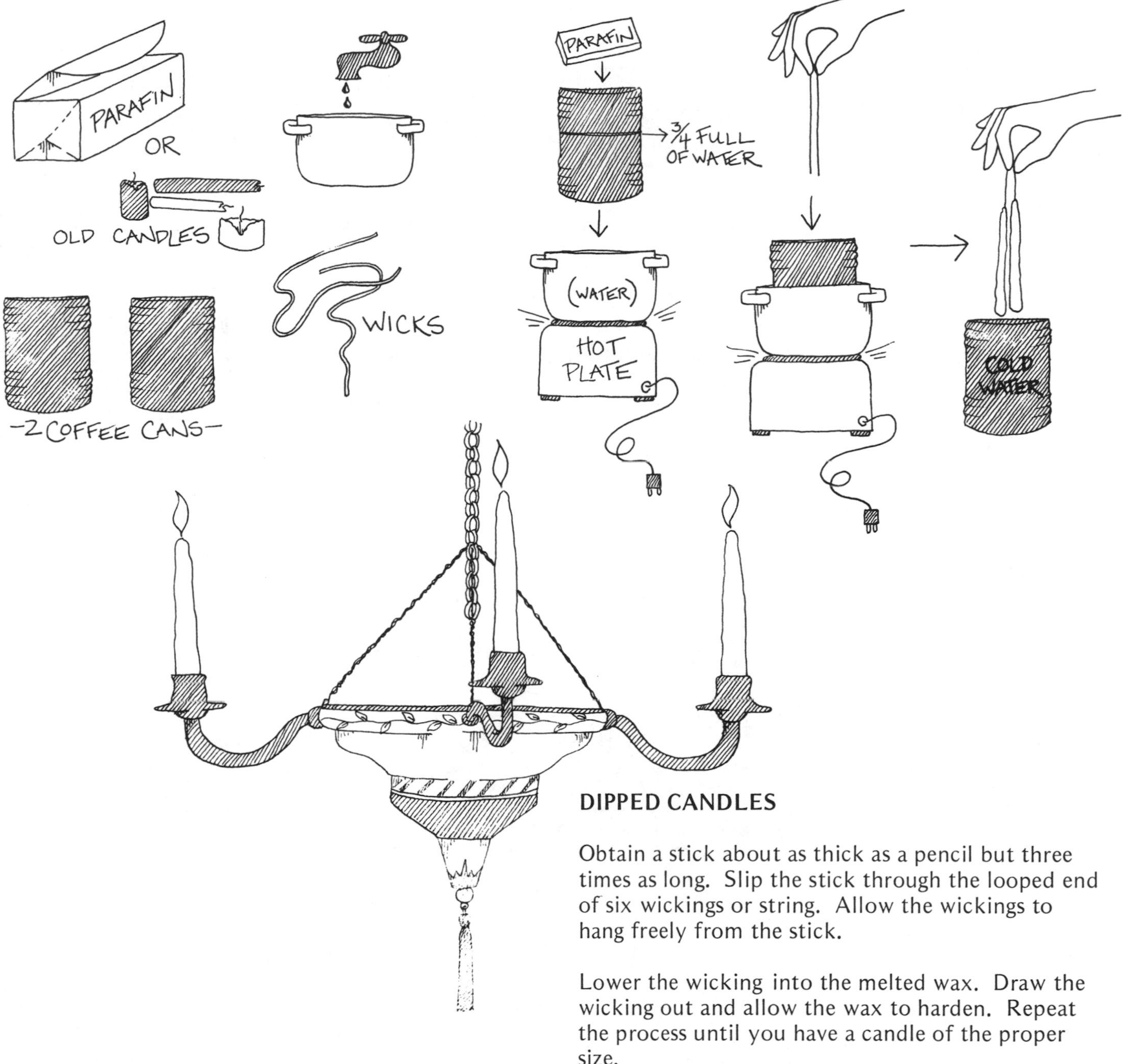

DIPPED CANDLES

Obtain a stick about as thick as a pencil but three times as long. Slip the stick through the looped end of six wickings or string. Allow the wickings to hang freely from the stick.

Lower the wicking into the melted wax. Draw the wicking out and allow the wax to harden. Repeat the process until you have a candle of the proper size.

If more than one candle rod is used, you can dip one set of wickings while the wax is hardening on the others. Use the safe and tidy methods in the pictures.

Materials — Paraffin or old candles
— Hot plate or stove
— Cans
— Water
— Wicking or thread

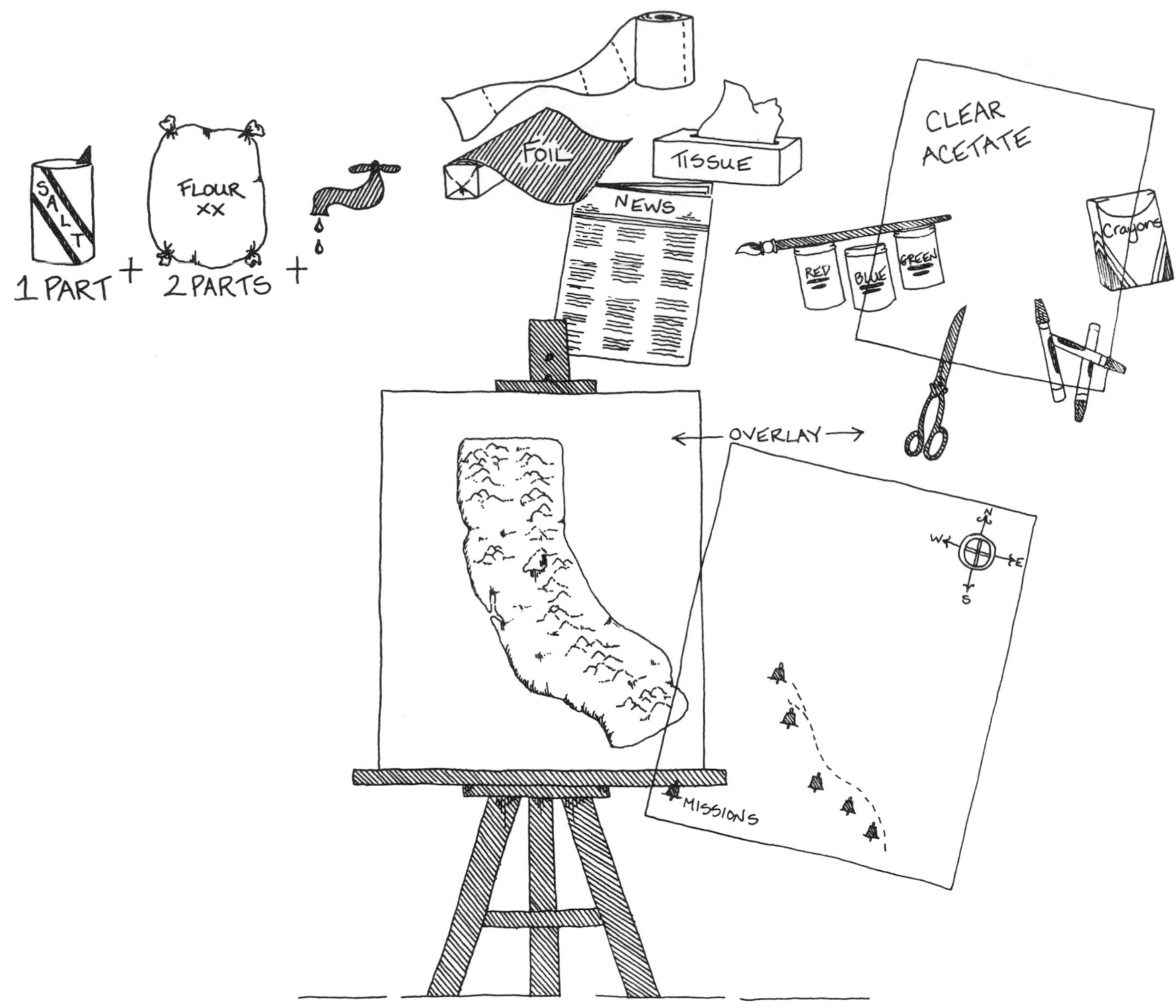

MAPS

Relief Maps

Relief maps may be made by using papier maché or a salt and flour mixture, as shown in the illustration.

Acetate-Overlay Map

Use crayons or marking pens on a clear piece of acetate to add detail; overlay on your basic map.

ADOBE BRICK MAKING

Use the materials, as shown, with 3 parts clay to 1 part sand and enough water to make a workable substance. Large wooden forms are used for big bricks. Big or little match boxes make fine molds depending on the projected size of your Mission.

Materials – Adobe clay
– Sand
– Water
– Straw for binding molds

PLANNING A CULMINATION INVITATION

Haul of Records

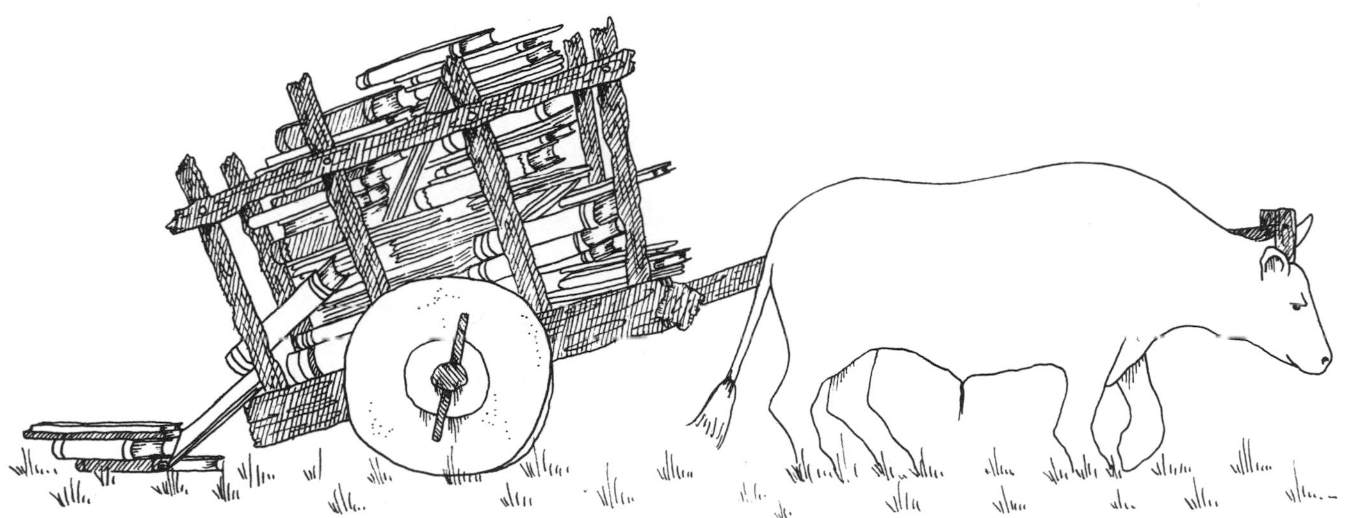

Time Line for Spanish California

Pre-Columbian until Columbus discovered the Americas

The California Indians lived in California from who knows when until 1769, undisturbed.

1492 – Columbus discovered America
1512 – Cortez came to Mexico
1521 – Magellan to Manila. The trading with the Manila galleons began.
1533 – Cortez to Baja California
1542 – Cabrillo explored the coasts of Baja and Alta California
1596 – Viscaino sailed up the coast of Baja California
1602 – Viscaino to Alta California
1615 – Captain Juan de Iturbi explored the Baja Peninsula
1683 – Father Kino and the Jesuits explored Baja Peninsula for future missioning
1697 – First Baja Mission founded by the Jesuits
1768 – The Franciscans came and the Jesuits left Baja
1769 – The Franciscans left Baja and went to Alta California and established Mission San Diego de Alcalá
1769 – 1824 – Twenty-one Missions established in Alta California
1834 – Secularization

Baja California Missions

Religious Order	*Mission*	*Founding Date*	*Present Condition*
Jesuit	Loreto	1697	Stone - rebuilt
Jesuit	San Javier	1699	Stone - good
Jesuit	Ligui	1705	Tile floor
Jesuit	Mulege	1705	Stone
Jesuit	Comondu	1708	Stone ruins
Jesuit	La Purísima	1719	Stone ruins
Jesuit	La Paz	1720	All gone
Jesuit	Guadalupe (Sur)	1720	Stone foundation
Jesuit	Dolores	1721	Adobe ruins
Jesuit	Santiago	1724	All gone
Jesuit	San Ignacio	1728	Stone
Jesuit	San José del Cabo	1730	All gone
Jesuit	San Miguel (Sur)	1730	All gone
Jesuit	Todos Santos	1734	Rebuilt - Adobe
Jesuit	San Luís Gonzaga	1737	Stone
Jesuit	La Pasión	1737	Stone ruins
Jesuit	Santa Gertrudis	1752	Stone
Jesuit	San Borja	1762	Stone
Jesuit	Calamajue	1766	Adobe ruins
Jesuit	Santa Maria	1767	Adobe ruins
Franciscan	San Fernando	1769	In ruins - Adobe as shown
Dominican	El Rosario	1774	Adobe ruins
Dominican	Santo Domingo	1775	Adobe ruins
Dominican	San Vicente	1780	Adobe ruins
Dominican	San Miguel de la Frontera	1787	Adobe ruins
Dominican	Santo Tomas	1791	Adobe ruins
Dominican	San Pedro Martir	1794	Stone foundation
Dominican	Santa Catalina	1797	Adobe ruins
Dominican	Descanso	1814	All gone
Dominican	Guadalupe (Notre)	1834	All gone

Mission Founding Dates

Mission	*Namesake*	*Founding Date*
San Diego de Alcalá	St. Didacus of Alcala	July 16, 1769
San Carlos Borromeio de Carmelo	St. Charles Borromeo of Carmel	June 3, 1770
San Antonio de Padua	St. Anthony of Padua	July 14. 1771
San Gabriel Arcángel	St. Gabriel the Archangel	Sept. 8, 1771
San Luís Obispo de Tolosa	St. Louis of Tolosa	Sept. 1, 1772
San Francisco de Asís *(also known as Mission Dolores)*	St. Francis de Asís	Oct. 9, 1776
San Juan de Capistrano	St. John of Capistrano	Nov. 1, 1776
Santa Clara de Asís	St. Clara of Asis	Jan. 12, 1777
San Buenaventura	St. Good Fortune	Mar. 31, 1782
Santa Bárbara	St. Barbara	Dec. 4, 1786
La Purísima Concepción	The Pure Conception	Dec. 8, 1787
Santa Cruz	St. Cross	Sept. 25, 1791
Nuestra Señora de la Soledad	Our Lady of Loneliness	Oct. 9, 1791
San José *(please pronounce Hosay)*	St. Joseph	June 11, 1797
San Juan Bautista	St. John the Baptist	June 24, 1797
San Miguel Arcángel	St. Michael the Archangel	July 25, 1797
San Fernando Rey de España	St. Ferdinand, King of Spain	Sept. 8, 1797
San Luís Rey de Francia	St. Louis, King of France	June 13, 1798
Santa Inés	St. Agnes	Sept. 17, 1804
San Rafael Arcángel	St. Raphael the Archangel	Dec. 14, 1817
San Francisco de Solano	St. Francis of Solano	July 4, 1823

Indian Games

THE INDIAN NUT-DICE GAME

Though this is mostly a woman's game among the Indians, it was widespread.

Materials:

— walnut shells, emptied and used as dice
— 200 sticks or teeny bones used as counters
— a basket to keep the materials in order

It's how you play the game that counts. Shake the shells in your hands and toss into a basket. Three up and three down gives the tosser 2 points; all tossed on one side gets 3 points. You get to take a stick or a bone for every point you make. Game is over when the sticks or bones are used up.

HAND OR GRASS GAME

Played by both men and women *(separate games)*

Materials: 2 pair of bones — one pair marked with sinew bands, other pair unmarked.
Players: Two players on each of two teams
Rule: Each person on one team has a pair of bones hidden in his hands
Scoring: Each member of the guessing team guesses which hand the marked bone is in.

Neither guess is correct — boneholders get 2 points
Both guesses are correct — guessers get 2 points
One guess right — guessers get one point, and incorrectly guessed boneholder takes another turn at hiding bones.

STICK GAME

Predominantly played by men

Materials: 44 sticks
Object: Correctly guess the remainder when the random number of sticks is divided into groups of four, i.e., 1, 2, 3, 4
Scoring: Number guessed correctly — guesser wins the sticks
Number guessed incorrectly — guesser lost bet (most probably given to him at 4-to-1 odds)

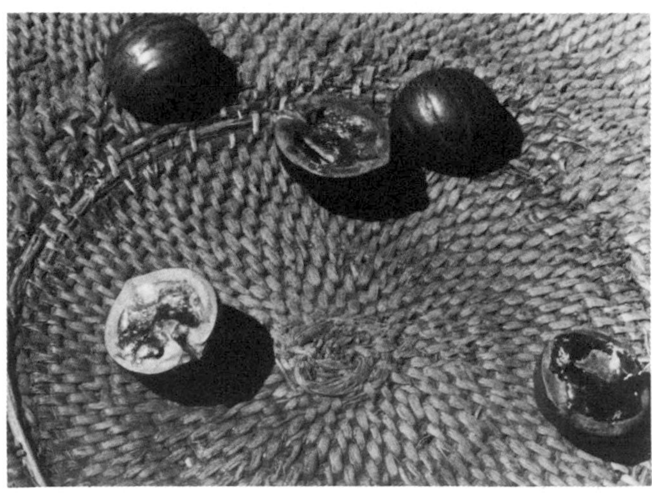

Products and Processes Brought to California by Spain

RANCHING AND ANIMAL HUSBANDRY:

Horses – Horsemanship, roundup, branding, lariat, rodeo, barbeque, stirrups, spurs, chaps, sombrero, corral
Cattle and Oxen – Meat, hides, tallow, candles
Burros and Mules – Riding, working, trading, hauling
Sheep – Mutton, wool, carding, spinning, weaving, sewing
Goats – Meat, milk, hair. Leaders for sheep
Chickens – Meat, eggs, feathers. Cockfights

AGRICULTURE AND HORTICULTURE

Introduction of grains – wheat, rye, oats, barley, rice *(and maize from Mexico).* Need for granaries, mills, millstones. Irrigation, cultivation, harvest. Calendar.
Alfalfa and hay crops – Forage for livestock. Tools for cutting, storage.
Vegetable gardens – Carrots, onions, garlic, lettuce, tomatoes, chiles, squash, peas, potatoes, yams.
Herb gardens – Peppercorn, marjoram, oregano.
Vineyards – Grapes, arbors, wineries, brandy distillation, Table grapes.
Olive orchards – Olive oil, presses *(rotary and upright),* storage jars.
Citrus – Oranges and lemons.
Fruit and nut orchards – Apple, peach, pear, fig, almond, walnut.
Irrigation – Ditches, reservoirs, aqueducts, fountains, techniques for raising water, wells.
The plow – Animal and human traction.
Transport of crops – Carretas, roads.

MARITIME ACTIVITIES

Fishing – Clams, crabs, salmon and ocean fish. Boats. Some European techniques and tools.
Sea otter. – Skins. Trade item. Techniques of harpooning. Aleuts imported by Russians and Yankees with their canoes.
Whaling – Oil, tusks.
Port facilities – Hide houses, docks, lighters.
Defenses – lighthouses.
Contact with Sandwich Islands*(Hawaii),* Mexico, China, Boston, England.

MISSION AND TOWN-BUILDING by:

Colonists: Padres and others
Retired soldiers
Christianized Indians
Foreigners

Mural made by children depicting trade in very early California

Make Mission Days Live

This activity is designed to inspire creativity and questions like *"How would I have done. . . .if I were there?"* Each group of children is supplied with an array of natural materials; for example, tules, bark, acorns, bones, black walnuts, soapstone, pictures of Mission pieces, etc.; and is asked to respond to a particular pressing problems. Response to such a problem helps each child realize the ingeniousness of the California Indians and early settlers' response to the same real life situations. "Pressing Problems" used successfully include: design a Mission, design a game, tell a legend, make a musical instrument, design a hunting technique, design a water vessel, design a grape press, design a mode of transportation. Any answer is acceptable, no matter how crazy it may seem.

This activity is very appropriate as an introduction to California history.

Mission Wall Words

On the walls of the Sonoma Mission, in large type, are the following words:

1. California's Mission system began at San Diego where Junipero Serra founded San Diego de Alcalá in 1769. Serra saw nine Missions established before his death in 1784.

2. With the padres came the soldiers, to protect the padres, neophytes and settlers. Some settlers brought wives from Mexico, others married Indian women.

3. Into the wilderness came the Franciscans; with plow and hoe and churchbell they settled in this new land.

4. From the beginnings of Christianity there have been Missions. California's twenty-one were Catholic. The history of the California Mission is beyond creed or sect. It is part of our heritage.

5. Beginning with bare earth and the padres' zeal, each Mission soon became a walled center of religion and general education for the Indians. Its pastoral husbandry encompassed a vast area of surrounding countryside.

6. California was the Spanish Crown's last frontier in America. Continuing a century-old system, the California Missions were a first step toward settlement of this frontier. They were to be followed by pueblos and ranchos.

7. Each Mission was an oasis, where the travelers could find safety, repose, and refreshment — a welcome sight in the wilderness.

8. The Mission grew from the very soil upon which it stood. Each had its own plan, following the ancient pattern of strong buildings in a fort-like arrangement about an open compound.

9. With materials native to each area and a few rude tools, the padres taught the Indian converts how to build the Missions. Using redwood, pine, oak, sycamore, soil and stone, they performed incredible feats of construction.

10. The Franciscans left a heritage and a great tribute to their labors. Catholic services have been restored to most of the Missions, and they function as churches and schools, except San Francisco Solano and La Purísima Concepción, which are state historical monuments.

11. Mexico won independence and carried the Spanish idea of secular churches to follow the Missions. Some became villages, churches, some were looted, some abandoned. Most came to a state of ruin.

12. Spaced a day's travel apart, from San Diego to Sonoma, California's Missions have been called "The Golden Chain." Twenty-one were founded between 1769 and 1823.

13. Mission San Francisco Solano — most of its buildings were gone,and later the earthquake of 1906 demolished what was left of them. Through the interest and effort of many persons over the past half century, the restoration you see today has been brought about.

Plant Tour

Around even the most urban areas grow many plants used by the natives of California. With a little background information, a short tour or display board could be used to describe some of these native plants and their California Indian uses. Also, an industrious group could begin a native plant use garden.

Suggested references include:

Balls. *Early Uses of California Plants.*
Sweet. *Common Edible and Useful Plants of the West.*
Murphey. *Indian Uses of Native Plants.*

Out of Food?

Make some acorn mush for breakfast, lunch, and dinner.

Grind acorns in a mortar with a pestle; put water into an Indian basket. Drop in some hot rocks for cooking, add acorn meal, and there it is! The Franciscans were so glad to know about this, too, because sometimes they ran out of grains,and they couldn't run to the store.

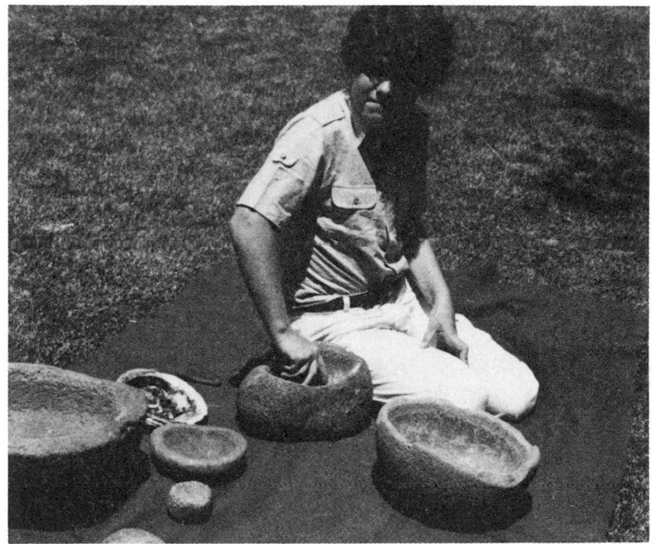

Architecture

Typical design was of a quadrangle, surrounding an open square with an enclosed chapel.

There were quarters for priests, Indians and the Presidio guard *(5-8 men)* – often together.

Kitchen and dining, office, library, workshops, classrooms, storage, laundry, stable, and punishment areas were fairly close together.

Architecture was Iberian and classic, modified, arch and dome, with tile roof, adobe walls, stucco, facade heavy beams. The overhang roofs were used to protect the walls. Embellished facade, windows with glass or parchment, bell tower, well or water storage, and barbecue pit were a part of almost every Mission.

DECORATION

The interior, was usually whitewashed, with wall design paintings, colored tiles, and wrought iron. There were carved pulpits, choir lofts, altars, tabernacles, fonts and water fountains, side chapels besides the main sanctuary of the church.

Religious Items

On display in many Missions are: altar cloths and hangings, priests' vestments, chalice and paten, wafer tongs, wine vessels, tabernacle, candles and candle holders, crucifix, missals, choir books, catechism books, musical instruments and bells, statues and images, paintings of saints and religious allegories, stations of the cross, incense, fireworks for fiestas, and baptismal fonts.

Also frequently displayed are: record books of marriages, baptisms, burials and deaths, etc.; religious books; linguistic books; and libraries.

Mission Processes

Bargaining

Trading can be an interesting activity. Appoint different children to different native or Mission groups and let them figure out where they live, who they might trade with, how far they might travel and the mode of travel, and what was the exchange, etc. Also notice the interesting correlations among Indian trade routes and El Camino Real and the present highway system. Check present harbors with barter ports of the past.

For more information:

Barrett, Gifford, and Davis. *Trade Routes and Economic Exchange Among the Indians of California.*
Dana. *Two Years Before the Mast.*

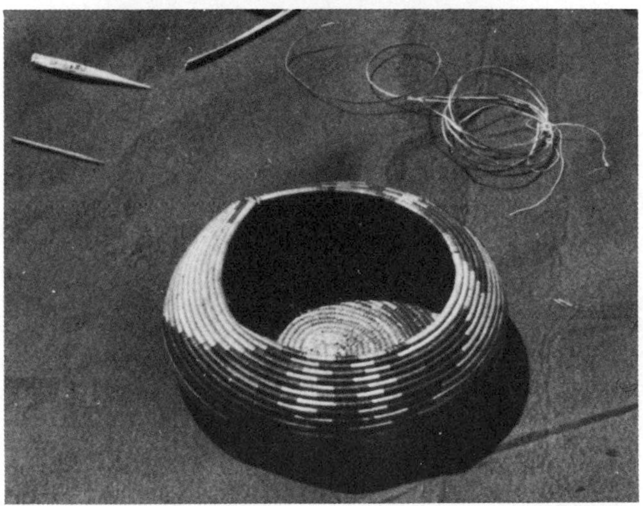

California Indian Baskets

California Indian baskets were made of many kinds of plant materials, from willows for the base and the weaving strands to combinations, including tules, hazels, and red bud.

The basket shape varied from Indian group to Indian group as well as did the decorative pattern.

The coil method was commonly used in basket making achieving a tight weave.

Take the wet willow or other base or warp materials and wind it into a circle or, yes, a coil.

With even stitches, weave the coiled pieces together. For this, use a tapestry needle and a slender piece of the willow or other native California plant.

As you build the side, simply continue adding willow warp and securing it with willow weft or other flexible material until you have the basket you wish.

To make a firmer basket, knot the weft *(weaving fibre between stitches).*

This is a mere beginning. Books, classes, films, and museums will furnish you with many more ideas on making baskets as the Mission and other California Indians did.

Parents, boys and girls, and teachers — write to the State Indian Museum, 111 I Street, Sacramento, California 95814, for more information. (Telephone *(916) 445-4204)*

Adobe Molds

Molds used for shaping the adobes are made of wood and may be lined with tin for a smooth surface. It prevents any sticking of the soil to the sides. Time will be saved if a double mold is prepared and two bricks can be made in a single operation.

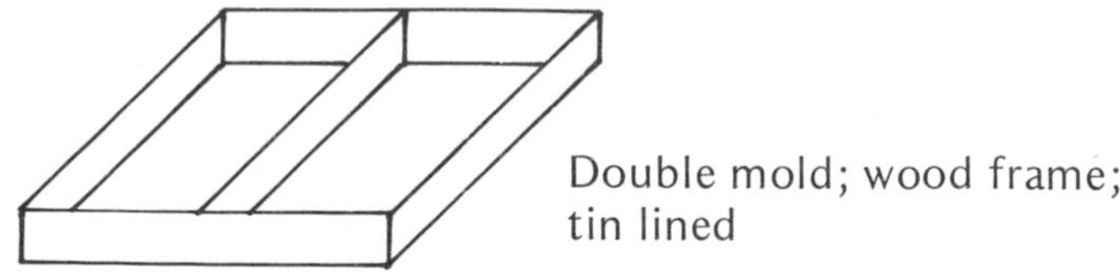

Double mold; wood frame; tin lined

Sun-Dried vs. Burnt Adobe

Some use is made of kiln-fired or burnt adobes. The outstanding advantage of burnt products are: the increased hardness due to the firing and the assurance that a thoroughly dry and very satisfactory adobe may be obtained in a relatively short time. A burnt adobe is very similar in color to an ordinary building brick and is very much harder than a sun-dried product.

Further, if a burnt adobe is left exposed to the natural elements it will remain unchanged for an indefinite period, whereas a sun-dried adobe, if exposed to rain, quickly "melts" and is soon a thin stream of mud. Burnt adobes, then, are resistant to weathering and can be made in a relatively short time.

On the other hand, the sun-dried bricks can be made at slightly less cost, and, if coated with plaster, cement, or stucco *(as is common in modern houses)* are not exposed to any weathering and will remain intact for many generations.

Preservation of Meat in Spanish California

Spanish Californians ate meat, but they had no refrigeration, so they preserved it by drying. This dried meat *(usually beef)* was called jerky or charqui.

Soap Making at the Mission

In Mission days, the process to make soap was long, because the lye had to be made from ashes and the tallow cut from a steer carcass. The modern method of soap making is as follows:

> 2½ pounds of tallow and one-half ordinary size can of lye; draw 3/4 pint of water; melt the tallow and then mix lye into water. **CAUTION: DO NOT SPILL LYE AS IT WILL CAUSE BURNS!** Mix lye-water and melted tallow together; stir until it begins to form into into soap. Pour into cookie cans, and let harden. Cut into bars.

The Carreta

The carreta was the cart that carried everything in Spanish California. It was pulled by a donkey, horse, or mule.

Make a carreta of cardboard and paint it as a model.

Mission Cooking

The Mission Fathers were not experienced chefs, but they managed the kitchens with the help of Neophytes. Breakfast was early, but probably after Mass. One family member from each Mission compound house came to the kitchen with a bowl and ladle to dish up the daily mush. Those Neophytes, who ate at the Missions, stood up to eat their mush. In the earliest days it was made from acorns, but wheat or corn were soon permanent substitutes.

Later, coffee or chocolate might be served around noon, but the largest meal was served about 2:00 PM in the dining room of the Mission.

One of the recipes included here might be the main dish. Honey was used instead of sugar. The main flavoring came from *chiles. Atole* was frequently served and might be part of *Cena* or supper with *tortillas.* Hot chocolate was the favorite drink.

The Mission Fathers not only prepared meals but raised the produce and animals and processed foods for the table. There were wine presses on the grounds, and slaughter houses from which the cows or sheep were taken at once for the tallow rendering and the hide tanning. Sausages, dried beef, dried corn, figs and apricots, and cheese were among the food stuffs grown and made on the Mission grounds.

While much of this was eaten at the Mission, hides and tallow were used for bartering with trade from the ships from Manila and Boston. The Mission Fathers sowed the seeds that have made California among the nation's largest in wine making, citrus fruit production and cattle raising.

Remember, as Spanish and Mexicans were the first newcomers to California, the earliest recipes are Spanish and Mexican.

Implements for Group Cooking: At home use the pots you have.

Crock pot: good for beans, rice or pasta soup
Oven pots
Skillet: *Tortillas, tacos, tostados; etc.*
Electric skillet
Food scales – if you have one available.
Tortilla holder: Fold a 2 lb. coffee can lid in two; use as a *tortilla* holder when frying *tortilla* in hot grease.

Spanish Mission Implements:

Wooden bean masher *(potato masher);* knives and boards for cutting *(a blender or food processor);* or lovely carved wooden chocolate mixer *(use slotted spoon);* cast-iron griddle for making *tortillas (electric frying pans and griddles);* Mexican lime squeezer *(orange squeezer, a blender or food processor);* wooden spoons of all sizes and shapes; *metate* and its grinding stone, *la mano* – the *metate* has 3 legs and is made out of rough volcanic rock and is sloping in form; a knife and cutting surface of some sort; a blender or food processor for grinding corn, *chiles* and all of the ingredients for making sauces. *Tortilla* press – or busy hands with a little ball of *Masa con Aqua* – these little balls are patted with hands always at right angles to each other, patting away and changing positions after every pat.

Remember, you can do Mission cooking with only one frying pan, minimum cooking ingredients and 25 to 30 pairs of hands. Don't hesitate to substitute *chiles* – but remember, the seeds and veins are very hot.

Spanish-California Recipes

NIXTAMAL

This is the base of many Mission foods as well as Mexican foods:

tortillas, tamales and tacos.

1 gallon water
1/3 cup unslaked lime
2 quarts *(8 cups)* whole dry corn *(maize)*
In galvanized kettle, mix the water and lime stirring with a clean stick or a wooden spoon. Add the corn and stir until the mixture no longer bubbles.
Bring to a boil, then lower the heat so that the mixture cooks but does not boil. Stir frequently. When the skins can be easily rubbed from the kernels *(after about one hour of cooking)* and the corn is moist through, remove from the heat.
Drain and wash in several changes of cold water until all trace of lime is removed. Rub the kernels between the hands until it is free of hulls.
You will have a clean corn much like hominy but not so well cooked. This is *nixtamal,* ready to be ground into *masa.*

Lime Water

Quick, or unslaked, lime is used in making the *nixtamal.* The ratio is 1/3 cup lime to 1 gallon water.

MASA

1 cup nixtamal
Water
Place one cup of *nixtamal* on a *metate;* sprinkle with water to keep it moist. With a small hand-stone, rub back and forth, over and over, until the corn kernels have formed a medium-fine dough. This is *masa.* Cover with a damp cloth to keep from drying.

TORTILLAS

IMPORTANT! The ever delicious *tortilla* now:

An *ENCHILADA,* fried in oil and all rolled up with filling and sauce;

A TACO, fried and folded, filled and sauced;
A TOSTADA, fried, flat, covered and sauced; and
A QUESADILLA, a little cheese, a little heat, and a little *tortilla.*

CORN TORTILLAS

Form the *masa* into 2-inch balls; press and pat with the hand into a 6-inch round cake. Bake on a hot, ungreased griddle until slightly brown and blistered on both sides.

Wheat Tortillas (Tortillas De Trigo)

2 cups *harina de trigo* (wheat)
¼ lb. lard or ½ lb. vegetable shortening
2 tsp. salt
1 cup warm water

Knead mixture for 3 minutes; set it aside for 3 hours before cooking.

QUESADILLAS

You can vary this recipe by adding beans, meat, onion, and/or garlic.

1½ cups Monterey Jack cheese, shredded *(or Cheddar cheese)*
6 Tbsp. green *chiles,* chopped
6 *tortillas*
Salt
Oil for frying

Put ¼ cup cheese and 1 tbsp. *chiles* on half of each *tortilla;* sprinkle each with salt. Heat a small amount of oil in a frying pan, and put the *tortillas* in, one at a time, without folding. Fry for a few seconds. Fold the *tortillas* over the filling, press the edges together. Fry on both sides until crisp. Drain on paper towel before serving. Makes 6.

TACOS

12 *tortillas*
3 cups lettuce, shredded
1 large tomato, sliced
1 large avocado, sliced
1 cup Cheddar cheese, shredded
½ pint sour cream
Pickled *chiles* to taste
Bottled green *taco* sauce to taste

Drop *tortillas* in hot oil, one at a time. After a few seconds turn, fold in half, and fry to desired crispness. Drain on paper towels and keep warm in a low-heat oven. To serve, open each *tortilla* gently and let each person select his own condiments. Serves 6.

TOSTADAS

8 *tortillas*
Oil for frying
2 cups refried beans
2 cups meat filling
2 cups shredded lettuce
2 sliced tomatoes
1 large avocado
½ cup Parmesan cheese
1 pint sour cream
8 ripe olives, sliced
Pickled *chile* slices

PRICKLY PEAR CACTUS PUNCH

Cactus juice
Sugar

Using the cactus juice for punch is quite delicious. It can be used full strength with a little sugar, or, can be "fizzed" with the addition of sparkling water or lemon-lime soda. Or, it can be added to any fruit punch that is made with a mixture of fruit juices such as lemon, lime, apple, or pineapple. One good punch is made with a weak tea base, adding cactus juice, lemon juice and a little cinnamon *(use a very light touch on the cinnamon).* As in any good punch, the mixtures should be made by adding juices a little at a time until it tastes "right."

SOPAIPILLAS

1 3/4 cups flour
1tablespoon salt
2 1/2 tablespoons double-acting baking powder
5 tablespoons chilled butter or shortening
2/3 to 3/4 cup milk
Cinnamon/sugar or honey

Sift the flour with salt and baking powder. Cut the shortening into the dry ingredients with a pastry blender until the mixture is the consistency of coarse cornmeal. Make a well in the center of these ingredients, add milk to make a slightly sticky dough, stirring just until mixed. Turn onto a lightly floured board, knead gently and quickly, 8 to 10 times. Roll with a lightly floured rolling pin to 1/4 inch thickness. Cut into 2 1/2 inch squares. Fry in deep fat at 400° until golden brown.

Roll in cinnamon/sugar or serve with honey or panocha.

ATOLE

This is a thick, hot drink, not unlike thin mush. It is enjoyed all over Mexico today as it was in the past. It was a favorite for Mission Fathers and Indians. There are many ways to make it: Mix a cup of corn flour *(masa)* or rice flour with 2 cups of cold water and a pinch of salt. To this add 2 cups of boiling water. Cook it oh, so slowly; for 1 hour.

For plain *atole* — Serve as is.
For spicy *atole* — add a little *chile.*
For fruit *atole* — add some fresh or canned fruit
For sweet *atole* — add a little brown sugar with cinnamon
For chocolate *atole* — add cinnamon, sugar and grated Mexican or bitter chocolate to the *atole* and you have and you made *champurrados* — or a "full bodied" hot chocolate.

Hot chocolate was very popular among Mission Members, Neophytes and Priests alike:
Chocolate beaters are available in Mexican food stores — they were used to fluff up chocolate cocoa. The chocolate was brought from Mexico on trading ships — squares of bitter chocolate are second to Mexico's own sweet chocolate "rounds." Milk, eggs, sugar, cinnamon can all be used in making Mexican hot chocolate.

SOPA DE CALABAZA

Pumpkin Soup

3 tablespoons lard
½ cup chopped onion
2 cloves garlic, crushed
2 tablespoons flour
3 cups chicken broth
2 cups milk
2 cups cooked, pureed pumpkin or Hubbard or Acorn Squash
1 cup whole kernel corn
1 tsp ground cumin
1 tsp salt
½ tsp pepper
1 egg yolk
1 cup cream
½ cup sherry
1 cup sour cream
1 cup toasted pumpkin seeds

Heat lard. Saute onion and garlic. Blend in flour. Add broth and stir until thickened. Add milk. Bring to boil. Lower heat or transfer to double boiler. Add pumpkin, corn and seasonings. Cook 20 minutes uncovered.

Beat yolk and cream. Add a little hot mixture, then then transfer to soup, beating with whisk until thickened, about 3 minutes. Add sherry.

Pour in bowls and top with sour cream and a sprinkling of pumpkin seeds.

EMPAÑADAS

These were made frequently in the Missions.

2 cups flour
2 tsp baking powder
1 tsp salt
½ cup shortening
1/3 cup ice water
Oil for frying

Sift flour with baking powder and salt, and cut shortening in with a pastry blender. Add water and knead lightly.

Divide mixture into 12 balls; roll each into a circle 1/8 inch thick. Put 1 spoonful of filling on half of each circle. Moisten edges of circles with water, fold over the filling, and press the edges together. Press fork tines around the edges. Bake in 400° oven for 20 minutes, until golden brown or fry in hot oil (300) until golden, and drain on paper towels. Makes 12.

TAMALES

Husks are sold by the pound. For 2 dozen *tamales* allow about 4 oz. Soak them in very hot water for about 15 minutes or until pliable. Separate the husks. Remove any corn silk, and wrap in a towel to dry. Foil may be used instead of husks. It is easier to handle the *tamales* if they are wrapped in cooking parchment paper even though they are in husks.

MASA *(the dough)*

3 cups *masa harina (prepared flour for making tortillas, etc.)*
1 cup shortening
2 cups chicken or pork broth, tepid
1 tsp. salt

Cream the shortening. Add part of the *masa harina* and salt. Cream. Add liquid then rest of *masa harina.* Beat until very fluffy. When sufficiently beaten a small ball of the dough will float in water.

Making the Tamales

Choose largest of the husks, or put two together, cementing them with a little of the dough. Be sure husk isn't too wet or the *masa* will not stick.

Spread a thick layer of *masa* on the wide end. Leave the pointed end empty. Put a generous spoonful of the red or green sauce on the *masa* and spread it. Put pieces of chicken, pork or beef or cheese *(shredded)* in center. Bring the two sides over, loosely. Turn up the pointed end. Tie with strip of husk or wrap in parchment paper, twisting the bottom end. Keep as nearly upright as possible.

TAMALE FILLINGS

Chicken Tamales

3 cups cooked chicken shredded very coarsely.
3 cups *salsa colorada,* preferably the one made with dried *chiles,* and cut the liquid down to 1 cup tomato sauce and 1½ cups water. Also add more cumin. If use the *salsa colorada* made with *chile* powder, thicken it with flour.

Pork Tamales

3 cups cooked pork in fairly large pieces
3 or 4 cups *salsa verde* made a little thicker by using little or no extra water.

Beef Tamales

3 cups shredded cooked beef
3 or 4 cups *salsa verde or salsa colorada.*

To fill the *tamale,* spread sauce over dough, then put in pieces of meat or fowl, then add more sauce. When it comes to serving, open up the *tamale* but leave it sitting on the husk. Add more sauce, kept aside for this purpose, and heated. Recipes for 12 *tamales.*

Variations: Instead of adding more *salsa colorada*

To fill the *tamale,* spread sauce over dough, then put in pieces of meat or fowl, then add more sauce. When it comes to serving, open up the *tamale*

Variations: Instead of adding more *salsa colorada* when serving, it is nice to top with *chili beans.* Cook beans as usual, rinse, then mix with *salsa colorado,* extra onions and cooked hamburger, if desired.

Add peanuts or almonds and/or raisins to the basic meat or chicken *tamale* recipes for a change of texture and taste.

COOKING THE TAMALES

The *tamales* must steam about 1½ to 2 hours in a kettle with a tight fitting lid. The kettle must be deep enough to hold about 2" of water below the rack on which tamales are placed. The *tamales* should be standing upright and the water must not touch them, but they must be arranged loosely so that the steam circulates around them. Put hot water in the kettle and place the rack so the water is below it. Arrange the *tamales* standing up on the folded end or twisted end if parchment paper is used. Put a cloth over the top of the kettle with the lid on top of the cloth. Keep the water boiling gently. Add water, if necessary, so that it won't boil dry. At the end of 1½ hours, take out a *tamale,*and unroll. If it is cooked the dough will come away from the husk and look and taste cooked. When serving the *tamale,* take off paper if paper is used, unroll husk and fold back under *tamale.* It is well to have some extra sauce hot to pour over the *tamale.*

SALSA COLORADA — Using *Chile* Powder

2 tablespoons lard
8 tablespoons *chile* powder
1 cup tomato sauce
3 cups water
1 tsp sugar
½ tsp ground cinnamon
Salt to taste

Melt lard. Add *chile* powder and cook, stirring, a few seconds. Add tomato sauce, simmer a minute or two. Add water and seasonings. Cook 10 to 15 minutes.

Taste for seasoning. You may wish to add more *chile* powder, or more cumin. The different brands of *chile* powder vary. When you have found one you like you will know what to add.

The *salsa colorada* made with the dried *chiles* has more body and seems to go farther. If you are making 12 *enchiladas* using the *chile* powder you might do well to increase the *chile* powder by 2 tablespoons and add 1 cup more water and 1 cup tomato sauce.

BUNUELOS Traditional Mission Dessert

Makes about 3 dozen

2 cups flour
¼ cup sugar
1 tsp. baking powder
1 egg
1/3 cup milk
2 tbsp. melted butter

Sift dry ingredients together. Beat egg and milk together. Add to dry ingredients. Add melted butter and mix well. Turn out on floured board and knead a few times. Wrap and chill if possible. Pinch off pieces about the size of a walnut. Roll into smooth balls. Roll out very thin, paper thin. Each one should be about 5" or 6" round. It is best to roll out all the *bunuelos,* stacking with paper between before you begin to fry them. Have oil very hot. Drop *bunuelo* in, turn, then turn again if not brown. Drain well on absorbent paper. While still hot, sprinkle with cinnamon and sugar. Traditionally they are served broken into bowls with Piloncillo syrup, and eaten with the fingers.

MEXICAN HOT CHOCOLATE

2 cups boiling water or 2 cups scalded milk
3 ounces Mexican chocolate, broken into small pieces

In a small heavy saucepan bring water to boil; stir in chocolate; mix over low heat, stirring until the chocolate is melted. Pour the mixture into an earthenware pitcher and whip it to a froth with a wooden *molinillo* or mix in blender for 2 to 3 seconds until frothy. Add cinnamon to make it fit for a party. Serves 2.

POZOLE – PORK AND HOMINY STEW

1 lb. pork neck bones
2 quarts chicken broth
½ cup chopped onion
3 or 4 cloves garlic
3 lbs pork cut in 1" cubes
6 oz. dried California *chiles* (about 12 pods) or 6 tbsp. *chile* powder
2 cups white hominy
1 cup cooked beans *(use ½ cup kidney beans cooked in 3 cups water.)*
Salt and pepper to taste

In large kettle cook neck bones in chicken broth, with onion and garlic, for about 2 hours. Remove neck bones, cut off meat, and return to kettle. Add pork cubes. Cook 45 minutes.

Remove seeds and veins from dried *chiles.* Soak in boiling water about 20 minutes. Drain. Puree.

At end of 45 minutes test to see if pork is done. Continue cooking if pork cubes are not tender. Add the pureed *chiles* (or *chile powder),* hominy, salt and pepper. Cook 15 minutes.

Serve in bowls with side dishes of:
chopped onions
oregano
lemon wedges
sliced radishes
salsa picante
shredded lettuce
chili pepper flakes

POZOLE (VEGETARIAN)

Early California Style

1 small onion, chopped
2 garlic cloves, chopped
Saute in:
1 tbsp. oil
Until brown, then add:
3 cups water or broth
½ cup raw kidney beans, washed
½ cup raw whole wheat berries or whole rye berries
1 tsp. mixed herbs
½ tsp. mustard seeds or mustard powder
¼ tsp. salt
¼ tsp. black pepper

Bring to boil; then cover and simmer for 1½ to 2 hours until tender. Add 3 to 4 large leaves of swiss chard, coarsely cut. Simmer about 10 minutes, until tender. Serves 2.

Vinegar – Put 2 gallons fresh water, a pint of dark molasses, and a dissolved yeastcake or powdered yeast packet all together in a wooden vat; cover with a thin sheet of cotton and Eureka! – in 3 or 4 weeks you'll have vinegar.

Spanish-English Dictionary (Glossary) for Spanish California

This might be called a starter glossary and can be reproduced for each user. As new Spanish words or the names of places are discovered, they may be added to this list.

If at all possible, have a Spanish-English Dictionary close at hand. They are available in libraries and inexpensive in book stores.

AN EVERYBODY GETS A COPY — GLOSSARY-DICTIONARY

The list of Spanish words chosen for inclusion in this glossary is far from complete. The words that are listed are frequently used Spanish words and many of these words pepper our state as the names of places.

SPANISH ALPHABET:

a b c ch d e f g h i j k l ll m n ñ o p
q r rr s t u v x y z

Some Pronounciation Hints:

a = ah e = ay as in May
i = ee, as in see o = o as in low
u = oo as in moo ch = ch as in choo choo train
rr = roll your r so you sound like an airplane just taking off or about ready to land
ll = ya ñ = like the n in Tanya

WRITTEN NUMBERS FROM 1 TO 20

uno, dos, tres, cuatro, cinco, seis, siete, ocho, nueve, diez, once, doce, trece, catorce, quince, diez y seis *(y means "and")*, diez y siete, diez y ocho, diez y nueve, veinte.

NAMES OF THE MONTHS

enero, febrero, marzo, abril, mayo, junio, julio, agosto, septiembre, octubre, noviembre, diciembre.

DAYS OF THE WEEK

domingo, lunes, martes, miércoles, jueves, viernes, sábado.

Adobe – special mud and straw mixture *(formed in a mold and dried in the sun or in an oven.)*

Agua – water; Agua caliente means hot water *(guess what the word is for hot)*

Ajo – garlic

Alabanza – the name of a Catholic song of praise, (alabado = praised)

Alba – morning prayer at the mission

Alameda – grove of poplar trees. Alameda is the name of a city, a county and many streets. Maybe you live on an Alameda.

Alamo –poplar tree: In California it is called the cottonwood tree. Alamo is the name of cities, streets, and schools, to name a few.

Alcatraz – Easter lily. Alcatraz was the name of a famous federal prison in San Francisco Bay. Also, a pelican.

Alhambra – a Moorish estate in Granada, Spain. The name of valleys, a city, streets and avenues in California.

Alto – high; upper; tall as "upper California" is higher up on the map than Baja California.

Amador – lover; sweetheart; Amador County, family, valley and town are all in California. Also, a man's name.

Amigo – friend

Ana – Santa Ana is a city near Disneyland. *(Ann, in English. St. Ann was mother of Mary, mother of Christ)*

Andreas – Saint Andrew; spelled "Andrés" a valley and an earthquake faultline.

Angel – angel; Los Angeles – The Angeles; short form of the city, El Pueblo de Nuestra; Senora La Reina de Los Angeles, "Our Lady the Queen of Angeles," California's largest city.

Antonio – San Antonio; Saint Anthony; a place, a ship, a name and a mission.

Anza – a Spanish explorer and expedition leader; also the name of a street; a desert, a park, and a train and a school or two.

Bahía – bay

Baja – lower; Baja California

Baño – bath; Los Baños – a bathing place of priests in earlier times; a city in California's cotton-farming country.

Barato – cheap; inexpensive

Bárbara – saint from Rome, Italy; in California: – a mission, Santa Barbara Channel Islands; a city; a county; the name of one of this book's authors.

Barca – a little boat made from tules, or just a little boat.

Barrio – a district in a city or town.

Bautista – baptizer; San Juan Bautista, "Saint John the Baptist;" name of a mission and a city, at least.

Bella – beautiful; many names of places contain this this word, such as Bella Vista which means " "beautiful view."

Bernardino – Saint Bernadette; a city and county named San Bernardino

Bienvenido – welcome

Boca – mouth, such as the mouth of a person, a bay, or a river.

Bolinas – an Indian name of a place.

Bolsa – pocket or purse; When the rancho period was in full swing, this word was often used to describe "a little piece of land."

Bonito – pretty; bonita; descriptive word or name of many pretty places.

Bota – a leather water or wine container.

Brea – tar, as in La Brea Tar Pits in Southern California.

Buena – good.

Buena Ventura – a good venture and the name of the 9th mission

Burro – beasts of burden; the original "carry-alls."

Caballero – horseman or gentleman

Caballo – horse

Cabra – goat

Cabrillo – a little goat; Cabrillo – name of California's early explorer.

Calabaza – squash

Calavera – skulls; the word Calaveras is the name of a California county.

Camino –Road; journey

Camino Real – King's Highway (real means "royal") "royal") which links the missions

Camino Alto – high road; the name of several streets.

Cañada – canyon; La Cañada is a town.

Carlos – Charles; El Rey Carlos de España (King Charles of Spain)

Cebolla – onion

Carpintería – Carpenter's shop; a town near Santa Barbara.

Carta – letter; Write one to your favorite mission today and, if you want an answer, be sure to put in a stamped, self addressed envelope.

Casa – house; casa grande – a large house; Casa Grande is a town.

Cerrito –a small hill; El Cerrito is a town in California

Chícharos – peas

Chico – young; Chico is a city in California.

Chiles – a very spicy vegetable used in Mexican cooking.

Chula Vista – a place in California; chula is beautiful or oh, so cute.

Cojo – a lame person; Cojo Point is a special valley.

Colorado – reddish; Colorado is a river and desert, also a state.

Comida – noon dinner

Conejo – rabbit; El Conejo is a rancho, a creek, and a mountain.

Coyote – a little North American wolf; Coyote River Canyon is a specific place.

Cruz – cross; Santa Cruz is the name of a city and county.

Cuesta – a hill.

Delgado – thin; Delgado Point is the name of a place. place.

Diablo – devil; evil; Diablo is a mountain; a college; and a valley.

San Diego – named for Saint Didacus. Say it fast 10 times and see if you can make it sound like San Diego!

Divisadero – a divider; Divisadero is a street name in San Francisco.

Dolor – pain; sorrow. Mission Dolores is often used as a substitute name for "Mission San Francisco de Asís."

Don – sir

Doña – madam

Dorado – golden; Eldorado is a county. You may find it in other places, such as on street signs.

El – the singular masculine article.

Estado – state

España – Spain

Fandango – Spanish dance

Felicidad — happiness; Felicidad is the name of a town.

Fierro — cattle brand to show ownership.

Fiesta — party; celebration; festival; holiday.

Flaco — thin

Flecha — arrow

Flor — flower; Las Flores is the name of many streets.

Fraile — friar; often used for priest

Fresa — strawberry

Fresno — ash tree

Frijoles — beans

Frío — cold

Fruta — fruit

Fuego — fire

Gallina — hen

Gallo — rooster

Garrote — house; capital punishment by hanging

Gato — cat; Los Gatos *(the cats)* is the name of a town.

Gaucho — herdsman or man of humble birth; later it seemed to mean "cowboy" in Argentina.

Gaviota — seagull; Gaviota Granada is the name of a town.

Guerra — war

Hacienda — large ranch

Hambre — hunger

Helado — ice cream

Hermana — sister

Hermano brother

Higo — fig

Hombre — man

Horno oven

Hornito (hornillo) — earth oven where Mexicans baked their bread; little oven.

Indio — Indian; Indio is a town in the desert area of California.

Santa Inés — Saint Agnes; A Mission and a river bear her name.

Isla — island

-ito, -illo — endings often put on the end of Spanish words to show that they are little or cute.

Jabón — soap

Jacinto — hyacinth; San Jacinto *(Saint Hyacinth; many mountains and ranchos are named for him.)*

Jardín — garden

Jitomate — tomato

Joaquín — a name from Catholic history; The name of a county, river, and valley.

La Jolla — the jewel; often mispronounced "joy a;" La Jolla is a city near San Diego. Should be spelled "La Joya."

José — Joseph; San Jose; Saint Joseph; San Jose is a city, and a Mission.

Juan Bautista — John the Baptist; Mission San Juan Bautista

Juan Capistrano — John; Mission San Juan Capistrano

Juego — game

La — the; singular, feminine article

Lago — lake

Laguna — small lake; Laguna Beach is a city.

Luís — Louis.

Madero — wood; Madera County.

Madre — mother

Malo — bad

Manteca — tallow; lard

Manzana — apple

Manzanita — little apple; reddish barked bush with red berries shaped like little apples.

Marina — adjective = marine; shore or coast; Marin may be the shortened form, as in Marin County, just north of the Golden Gate Bridge; and the home of Mission San Rafael. Small harbor for boats.

Marinero — sailor

Mayordomo — person in charge of vaqueros or cowboys

Mesa — table; level hill

Mestizo — Indian and European heritage.

Metate — Indian grinding stone; this is like a mortar and pestle, which is a round grinding rock with rock instrument to do the grinding; used by the Indians.

Miguel — Michael; San Miguel — a saint, a mission, and a little town.

Modesto — modest; Modesto is the name of a city

Montar — to ride horseback.

Monte — mountain; used in naming many places, such as El Monte; Montecito *(see how many streets, little towns or big towns have this as their first word).*

Morro — animal snout or round hill; headland; cliff; Morro Bay and rock.

Muerto — dead; also used in the names of places hither and thither

Mujer — woman

Nacimiento — birth; name of a river and a canyon

Nada — nothing; Nada is a place, too.

Naranja — Orange

Natividad — the birth of Christ at Christmas. Also Navidad.

Nevada — snow-covered; the Sierra Nevada mountain range; Nevada County and the state of Nevada.

Niño — child

Noche — night

Noche buena — good night or Christmas.

Novato — a beginner; Novato is a town.

Nuestra — our

Nueva — new

Nuez — nut; especially pecan.

Obispo — bishop

Océano — ocean

Ojai — an Indian place name and a city near Santa Barbara.

Ojos — eyes

Olivero — basket for carrying olive from harvest to storage.

Olivo — olive or olive tree.

Olvera — a Spanish — California leader and a famous street in Los Angeles.

Pablo — Paul; San Pablo — Saint Paul; a bay and a city.

Pacífico — peaceful; our ocean's name.

Padre — father; priest; Los Padres — a national forest near Santa Barbara.

Pais — country

Pájaro — bird; Pajaro is a river and a valley.

Palo – stick; Palos Verde – Green Stick; Palo Alto is a city.

Paso –pass; passage; Paso Robles – Pass of the Oaks.

Piñata – a clay pot usually decorated with paper frills and filled with goodies for parties.

Piñón – pine nuts; the name of a place or two; Pinon Point; Punta de Pinon

Pismo – Indian place word meaning tar.

Playa – beach; Playa Del Rey is a place and the name of a beach; beach of the king.

Plumas – feather or a pen *(remember, they used to use feathers as pens);* There is a county named Plumas and a river named Feather. Now that's a switch!

Portola, Gaspar – the Spanish commander of the expedition that explored and colonized California; a city, valley, street, and maybe more. Look for this name in your community.

Potrero – a field that was or is used as a pasture for horses. You'll see it on street signs in a few cities.

Presidio – military location.

Pueblo – village

Pulga – flea; There must have been lots of early scratchers because streets and valleys and other places have Pulga in their names.

Punta – point; The early namers used this. See how many puntas there are in your area.

Purísima – purest; Mission La Purísima was named for Mary, the mother of Jesus.

Queso – cheese

Rafael – St. Raphael the Archangel; his name was used for a Mission, a city and a rancho.

Rancho – ranch really refers to the big cattle - raising ranchos during the cattle raising days of Spanish and Indian California; started, of course, by the Mission founders.

Rata – rat

Real – royal; later, when we were not under "royal or kingly" rule this meant "open." El Camino Real was named the King's Highway by the Spanish who had a king but now the "kingly" meaning is ~~lsot~~ in a lovely sea of democracy.

Redondo – round; Redondo Beach must be a round beach!

Refugio – refuge; shelter; Refugio is at least the name of one rancho and one playa or beach.

Reina – queen

Represa – repressed; the name of the post office for the prison and town of Folsom; a small dam.

Rey – king

Rincón – corner

Río – river; name of towns on river banks, creeks, and rivers. Be on a "río" search!

Rodeo – a cattle roundup; today a rodeo often is a great big show including competitions, contests, etc., for the public, showing cows, steer, horses, etc. at their show-off best; it still means a cattle roundup.

Rosa – rose; Santa Rosa was a Peruvian saint and is the name of a city and other palce names.

Rubio – blonde

Sacramento – sacramento; Sacramento is the name of California's capital city; a county; and a river.

La Sala – living room

Salina – a salt pit or marsh; Salinas is a city, a river, and a valley near Carmel and Monterey.

Sandía – watermelon

Santa – Saint

Sausalito – little willow grove; Sausalito is the name of a Golden Gate Bridge town, possibly taken from little willow.

Seguro – safe; sure

Señor – sir; gentleman; mister.

Señora – mistress; lady; madam

Sepulveda – name of many locations, i.e., pass, boulevard; Sepulveda is a Spanish surname.

Serra, Junipero – the first President of the California Mission System and a highway.

Silla – chair

Silla de Montar – saddle

Sitio – location

Socorro – help

Sobrante – left over; El Sobrante is a place near San Francisco built on extra land.

Solano – a place with lots of sun; name of an Indian chief and the name of a county; Mission San Francisco Solano in Sonoma County.

Soldado – soldier

Soledad – solitude; Soledad is the name of a city and prison; Mission Nuestra Senora de la Soledad.

Sombrero – a large brimmed hat.

Sonoma – an Indian name for General Vallejo's settlement; a county; city and a state park.

Sueño – sleep; dream.

Sur – south; Big Sur.

Tamal – name of Indian tribe.

Tamal País – country of the Indian tribes; pais means country. A mountain.

Tejón – badger; El Tejon is a specific pass and a canyon.

Temblor – earthquake

Término – end

Tía – aunt

Tío – uncle

Tiburón – shark; Tiburon is a peninsula, ranch and a town on the San Francisco Bay.

Tierra – land or earth.

Timoteo – Timothy; San Timoteo – Saint Timothy; Marin County Land Grant

Trinidad – trinity; Trinidad is a bay, a town, a county, and a river.

Triunfo – triumph; Triunfo is a canyon and a pass.

Trocar – to barter and/or exchange; tallow and hides were used as barter for needed goods. These were brought from the far east and the Eastern United States.

Trueque – to barter and/or exchange; tallow and hides were used as barter for needed goods. These were brought from the far east and the Eastern United States.

Tulare – a grove of bullrushes; Tulare is a city and county.

Tuna – a prickly pear cactus.

Último – last

Un – one (masculine - adjective form)
noun = uno.

Una – one (feminine)

Usted – you

Uva – grape; name of a canyon and the "Grapevine" is the name of a curvy highway.

Vaca – cow; name of a Spanish family; Vacaville – cow city

Valle – valley; the big central valley was named el valle grande.

Vallecito or Vallejo – a little valley; Vallejo – a Mexican military leader and land owner; the name of a city usually said Valeho.

Vaquero – cowboy

Vega – open plain

Vela — candle

Venida — arrival

Venta — sale

Ventana — window

Ventura — fortune or luck; Mission Buena Ventura

Verdad — truth

Verde — green; Verde appears in the names of many California places.

Viento — wind

Villa — village or country house.

Visitación — Visitation; Visitacion is a rancho and a valley.

Vista — view; part of the names of many places, i.e., Vista del Mar is "view of the sea;" Linda Vista is "beautiful view."

Viva — long live; hurrah.

W — No initial "w" in Spanish.

Yerba — herb; Yerba buena is "good herb;" name of a place and an island in San Francisco Bay.

Glossary Extension

Corte Madera – cut wood

Lagunitas – little lagoon

La Purisima – the pure one

Salinas – salty

San Bernardino – Saint Bernard

San Carlos – Saint Charles

San Francisco – Saint Francis

San Mateo – Saint Matthew

Santa Barbara – Saint Barbara

Santa Inez – Saint Agnes

Sonoma – an Indian word used for Vallejo's home area

Tia Juana – Aunt Jane, Tijuana, a Mexican border town

Trinidad – trinity

Vallejo – Mariano Guadalupe, Mexican land owner and military leader

Bibliography

The Annotated Romona. Wide World Publishers, Box 476, San Carlos, CA 1989.

Arillaga. *Diary of His Surveys of the Frontier* - 1766. Translated into English--1969.

Barton, Bruce. *A Tree in the Center of the World.* Ross Erickson. Adult. Very complete volume on the Missions with charming folk tales used hither and yon to make the time come to life. Do have a copy around.

Bauer, Helen. *California Mission Days.* Doubleday & Co. Good children's book on the settling, working in, and living in the California Missions. This book is so complete that it serves all ages.

Bauer, Helen. *California Rancho Days.* Doubleday & Co. All ages. Manner of rancho acquisition discussed together with the mode of rancho life. Particular "features" of a number of separate ranchos are delightfullly dealt with; a good glossary and a "Rancho Guide Table" is available for use.

Bernstein, Margery and Krobin, Janet. *Earth Namer.* Charles Scribner & Sons. A California Indian myth.

Biggs, Donald. *Conquer and Colonize.* Presidio Press. Level: adult and gifted children.

Caduto & Bruchac, *Keepers of the Earth*, Fulcrum, Inc. Golden, Colorado, 1989.

California Historical Landmarks, Office of Historic Preservation, California Department of Parks and Recreation. 1990.

Castor, Henry. *The First Book of The Spanish-American West.* Albert Micale, Illustrator. Level: 4th grade to adult. Wonderful pictures show the Indians and their successors, the explorers. The missionaries, the "support goups" of Spanish California are put into the total context of the history of California.

Coolidge, Dane. *California Cowboys.* University of California Press, 1985.

Copely, James. *The Call to California.* Union Tribune Publishing Co. Level: grades 7 and up. This book tells the story of the 1769 Portola/Serra expedition. Father Crespi's delightful diary is tucked in bits and pieces to set the work on fire a bit. Well illustrated.

Dakin, S. *Three Women of Spanish-California.*

Dana, Richard Henry Jr. *Two Years Before the Mast.* A personal history. This is truly a classic and offers the reader fine literature and craftsmanship, compelling descriptions of life on and off a Boston trading ship. Bartering on the Spanish-California Coast comes to life.

DaSilva, Owen Francis. *Music of California.* The Mission Fathers discovered a delightful method of instructing Mission Indians in part singing, through the use of colored music notes. Mission Santa Barbara houses many of these lovely sheets and Father DaSilva was the real Mission musicologist.

de Angulo, Maime. *Indian Tales.* Hill and Wang.

Duffus, R. L. and Norton. *Queen Calafia's Island.* Level: easy adult. Fine background reading with legend and fact, placing Spanish Alta and California missionaries in the totality of the state's earliest footsteps until today. *Queen Calafia* is a very fitting title as we glimpse into the whys and what fors of naming the state. This book lacks bibliography and an index.

Denevi & Maholy, *Junipero Serra*, Harper Row. 1985.

Eargle, Delan. *The Earth is Our Mother, Our Mother Delan Eargle.* Trees Press, 49 Van Buren, San Francisco, CA 94131, 1986.

Englehardt. *The Franciscans of California. Missions and Missionaries of California.* A dedicated researcher and author. Level: adult. Probably the best work, certainly up to its publication in 1916. You can learn a lot from Father Engelhardt.

Farber & Lasagne. *Whispers Along the California Indian Trails* and *Whispers along the California Mission Trails.* Magpie Press, San Ramon, California. Student's Edition and Teachers' Editions. 1983 and 1988.

Geiger, Maynard. *Life and Times of Father Junipero Serra.* This is another calssic resource written by a Franciscan.

Hawthorne, Hidegard. *California's Missions: Their Romance and Beauty.* Level: adult. This doesn't belie the title for indeed this "romance" may have more "glitter" today than at the time of their founding. A book to catch you up in all the best of Spanish California.

Heizer & Elasser. *The Natural World of the California Indian.* U. C. Press. Adult. The book is divided into topic areas which are then dealt with regionally. this contains excellent background reading.

Hutchinson, W. H. *California the Golden Shore by the Sundown Sea.* this is a very complete paper back history of California. Spanish California is discussed fully and is like a diamond in taking its place in a bracelet. It neither dominates nor is dominated by any other historical era. This is a real ready reference.

Jackson, Helen Hunt. *Ramona. Father Juipero Serra and the Mission Indians. Glimpses of California and the Missions.* Little, Brown. 1902. the first two of these and the Mission Collection of little Mission stories are literary classics of the time, but surprisingly, if used alone, today would evoke much controversy, i.e., could be a maudlin approach to those "precious" Missions and missionaries.

Karney. *The Listening One.* John Day. For children. This is the story of a California Mission Indian girl. It is the sotry of her tasks, her life, her struggles and her victories. It is set in the background of the Spanish-Mexican struggle over California.

Leeper, Vera. *Indian Legends Live In Puppetry.* Naturegraph. A creative manual.

Lewis, Oscar. *The Story of California.* Doubleday. Level: grade 4 and up. The chapter headings: Discovery; Drake and the Golden Hinde; Manila Galleons; Trail-Breakers; Missions and Ranchos; The Coming of Foreigners; etc. give an indication of the scope of this work. This book is well conceived, well written and illustrated and gives a good background.

Marinacci. *California's Spanish Place Names.* Presidio Presss. All ages. This is a charming book that bounces the reader all over California on street and highway signs. Little stories perk up the reader's understanding of the Spanish starter words in California.

Martinez, Pablo L. *A History of Lower California.* An English translation.

Michaelis, John. *Social Studies for Children in a Democratic Society.* Prentice Hall. Dr. Michaelis gives the reader a solid, worthwhile foundation on which to place the social studies education of our K-12 population. Keep a copy at your elbow.

Newcomb, Rexford. *The Old Mission Churches and Historic Houses of California.* Lippincott. Level: adult. This is a treasury of Mission and Mission style architecture. It doesn't simply present the reader with examples and descriptions but expands to include sound arguments for Mission Architecture in California.

Palver, Francisco. *Founding the First California Mission.* Nurvena California Press. Level: adult. This is truly an "I was there" account of the founding of the early Missions. Good primary source material.

Pitt, Leonard. *The Decline of the Californios.* University of California Press. 1989.

Robertson, *Baja California and Its Missions.*

Rush, Phillip. *Some Old Ranchos and Adobes.* Level: adult or gifted. A number of these "early sites" are described in detail. Differences and similarities of many ranchos are pinpointed. Good reading for the history buff.

Scott. *Junipero Serra -- A Pioneer of the Cross.* Valley Pub. This is for children. It is the story of the boy who became the man who started our California Mission system.

Sunset. *The California Missions.* Land Publishing. This is an outstanding book, from exploration to secularization. It is very complete and is recommended as a general reference book on the Missions.

Towendolly, Grant (tales told to) Masson, Marcelle. *A Bag of Bones.* Naturegraph. Legends of the Wintu Indians of Northern California.

Wheelock and Guillock. *Baja California Guidebook* -- 1975. Clark. The authors have included sections on the history and georgaphy of Baja as well as sections on travel and plant and animal life.

Bibliography of Early California Educational Resources

Beoule, Mary Null. *The Missions*, 21 books, one on each mission. 1988. Excellent resources for mission reports and mission model making. Tioga Publishing Company, Tahoe City, CA 1991

Gleason, Duncan. *Islands of California — Their History Romance and Physical Characteristics*. 1950. the author is the artist and this volume is worthwhile to look for in libraries.

California's Landmark. Office of Historical Preservation and Departments.

California History: A Quarterly Journal published by the California Historical Society. 678 Mission Street, San Francisco, CA 94105. The Fall 1995 issue is devoted to Mexican Americans in California.

Canfield, Chauncy. *The Diary of a Forty-Niner*. 1992. The story of life of a forty-niner from 1850 in California. The delightful original letters transport the reader to another time.

Holliday, J. S. *The World Rushed In: The California Gold Rush Experience*. Simon & Schuster. 1983. The original letters set between members of a family separated by the Gold Rush. An incredible primary source account of "Westward Ho" and "Life Back Home."

Hollister, Jane. *The Ranch Papers*. Wheelwright Lapis Press. 1988. The author describes a California rancho in the early 20th Century.

Linse, Barbara. *California's Hispanic Roots for Kids, las Raíces hispanas de California para los niños*. Art's Publications, 80 Piedmont Court, Larkspur, CA 1995. Wonderful new bilingual resource for girls and boys in Spanish and English.

Nadeau, Remi. *Ghost Towns and Mining Camps of California, A History and Guide by Crest Publishers*, Santa Barbara, CA 1992. Some better fourth grade readers will eat this up. The stories begin with the time of blending the Hispanics and the Gold Fever Cultures. Family and school field trips are natural outcomes of this sprightly book.

Whizz-Bang — Favorite stories of California's Past. Dr. History's Favorite Stories of Californis's Past.

Arts and Crafts Books

Arts and Crafts for All Seasons, Linse (Simon & Schuster)

Paper Construciton for Children, Krevitshy *(Rheinhold)* This book can point your way to mission people, animals, and growing things with paper construction.

Weaving Witnout a Loom, Rainy *(Davis)*

The Art of Papier Maché, Kenny *(Chilten)*

Making Things, Wiseman *(Little Brown)*

Creating with Paper, Johnston *(University of Washington)*

Mask Making, Baranski *(Davis)*

Cook Books

California Mission Recipes, Cleveland, Bess *(Tuttle)*

California Rancho Cooking, McMahan, Jacqueline Higuera. 1984 *(The Olive Press)*

Cooking With a Mission, La Purisima Mission State Historic Park. 1990

The Cuisines of Mexico, Kennedy, Diana *(Harper and Row)*

30 Mexican Menus, Stone, Idella Purnell *(The Ward Ritchie Press)*

The Complete Book of Mexican Cooking, Oritz, Elizabeth Lambert *(Bantam)*

The Mexican Cook, Wallace, George & Inger *(Nitty Gritty Productions)*

Mexican Cooking, Fisher, Kathleen Dunning *(Grosset & Dunlap)*

Instructional Materials

Basketry of the Pomo
U.C. 21 minutes. Color
Shows, through slow motion, some shapes and methods of making Pomo Indian baskets.

Basketry of the Pomo
U.C. 33 minutes.
The techniques of forming and decorating baskets is shown in some detail.

Basketry of the Pomo – Techniques
U.C. 30 minutes.
This film shows the California Pomo Indian women gathering and preparing the material, including feathers and beads, for their basket making. They are shown demonstrating some techniques.

Candle Making
Barr. 11 minutes.
The dipping method of making candles is shown in some detail.

California
Oxford Films. 12 minutes.
An overview of California's history and geography are given. This is a good background builder.

California Dawn
Consolidated Films. 27 minutes. Color
California's history from Cabrillo's discovery to the signing of the constitution.

California's Geographical Regions
Barr. 11 minutes. Color
The six regions are shown, compared and contrasted: North coast, south coast, Sierra Nevadas and the Central Valley. This helps all who view it to understand better the topographical differences and similarities of California.

California – Geography, Weather, Water
Avis. 20 minutes.
A broad overview of geography, weather and water is shown as they interact.

California Missions
R.K.O. 10 minutes.
This film shows the Mission trail and traces the history and development of the Mission to show their purposes. Missions are shown past and present.

California Picture Book
United World. 9 minutes.
The Monterey Peninsula, Santa Barbara, Los Angeles, and the giant redwoods are shown in their dramatic glory.

The Dream That Became California
Cypress. 18 minutes. Color
This film gives a brief historical account of Spanish life in California, particularly of the Mission system.

The Indians of California, Parts I and II
Barr. 29 minutes.
Trading, cradle and basket making, house building, deer hunting, gathering and preparing acorns are among the aspects of California Indian life shown.

Mission Life
Barr. 22 minutes.
The daily activities of the Mission Native Americans are pictured as they were at their height. The narration is by a padre writing in his journal.

Missions, Ranchos and Americans
Oxford Films. 14 minutes. Color
California's roots are shown through such sources as a diary and the period folk art. The heart of the film is the Spanish beginnings of California.

Missions of California #1 – Mission San Gabriel
Archangel
C.T.C. (1989) 10 minutes. Color
Approximately nine miles east of Los Angeles stands the fourth California Mission. We learn how the missions became the center of the Spanish culture in California.

Missions of California #2 – Mission San Diego De Alcala
C.T.C. (1989) 10 minutes. Color
The story of the first of nine missions founded by Father Junipero Serra. This mission was the first of 21 and the first permanent settlement in California.

California's Golden Beginnings
CALCOM. 22 minutes (1949) Color
Traces the development of the "golden" state from its early beginnings to the present.

California's Heritage
ALAMEDA (1970) 16 minutes. Color
Review of California's history showing origin, pre-history, coming of Native Americans, explorers, Spanish settlers and the Gold Rush era. This film then focuses on four factors affecting California's growth since the 1950's (1) water, (2) transportation and communication (3) industry, (4) people.

California's Heritage
NBVC. 16 minutes. Color
Presents California's history as a continuous, living process. Focuses on four factors affecting California's growth – water, transportation and communication, industry and people.

California (Spanish)
OF. (1974) 12 minutes. Color
Photography and potpourri of geographic and historical concepts successfully convey the contemporary flavor of San Diego, Los Angeles, and San Francisco. A typical ghost town and a chain of missions along El Camino Real provide a look at its past.

California Centennial
STOILC (1948) 15 minutes. Color
Part 1 covers the early Spanish-American era and the Missions, the gold rush, and Sacramento, San Francisco Bay Area, Redwood Highway and points in Northern California. Part 2 takes a trip through the great Central Valley, Yosemite, Los Angeles Basin and Southern California.

California Dreams: The Dream of Don Guadalupe
KQED. 30 minutes. Color
Documents the life of Mariano Guadalupe Vallejo through his writings in the Historia de California and personal letters. Covers the history of California from 1771 to 1890.

California History: On Location: California Recuerdo
KQED. 20 minutes. Color
Old Town in San Diego – Highlights the Mexican heritage of the Californios Era, 1822-1848.

Missions of California #3 – Mission San Juan Capistrano
CTC. 10 minutes. Color
The story of the most-visited mission in California, famous for the swallows that return every year and a rare look at California's oldest building.

Missions of California #4 – Mission Santa Barbara
CTC. (1989) 10 minutes. Color
Story of the "Queen of the Missions," the 10th mission and the first to be founded by Father Serra's successor, Father Fermin Lausen.

Missions of California #5 – California's Heritage: The Mission
CTC. (1989) 10 minutes. Color
An overview of how the missions began and the interaction between the two cultures; the original Native Americans and the Franciscan Padres from Spain.

Missions of California #6 - Mission Indians
CTC. (1989) 10 minutes. Color
Shows an overview of how the missions affected the lives and heritage of the Native Americans who first inhabited California.

Missions of California #7 - Class Project: The Making of a Mission
CTC. (1989) 10 minutes. Color
Students on location at a mission are shown building adobe bricks just as mission Native Americans did hundreds of years ago: also, model structures of various missions made by students are displayed.

Weaving Looms You Can Make
A.C.I. 16 minutes.
Simple homemade looms are shown which might turn your children into a weaving group of Mission Native Americans.

Native American Life – Check with a school materials center for producer and availability of these films:

Concow – (Film about the Concow Indians includes much plant use information.)

Acorns and Buckeyes – (Effectively presents the food processing of leaching etc.)

Bryan Beavers – (Film about an old timer and his particular life style.)

Bolton, David. Video. *Inside the California Mission.* Order from educational Book Distributors, Box 551, San Mateo, CA 94401 Phone 1-800-761-5501 . Through this video kids are taken into each Mission on a talking tour. It is highly recommended.

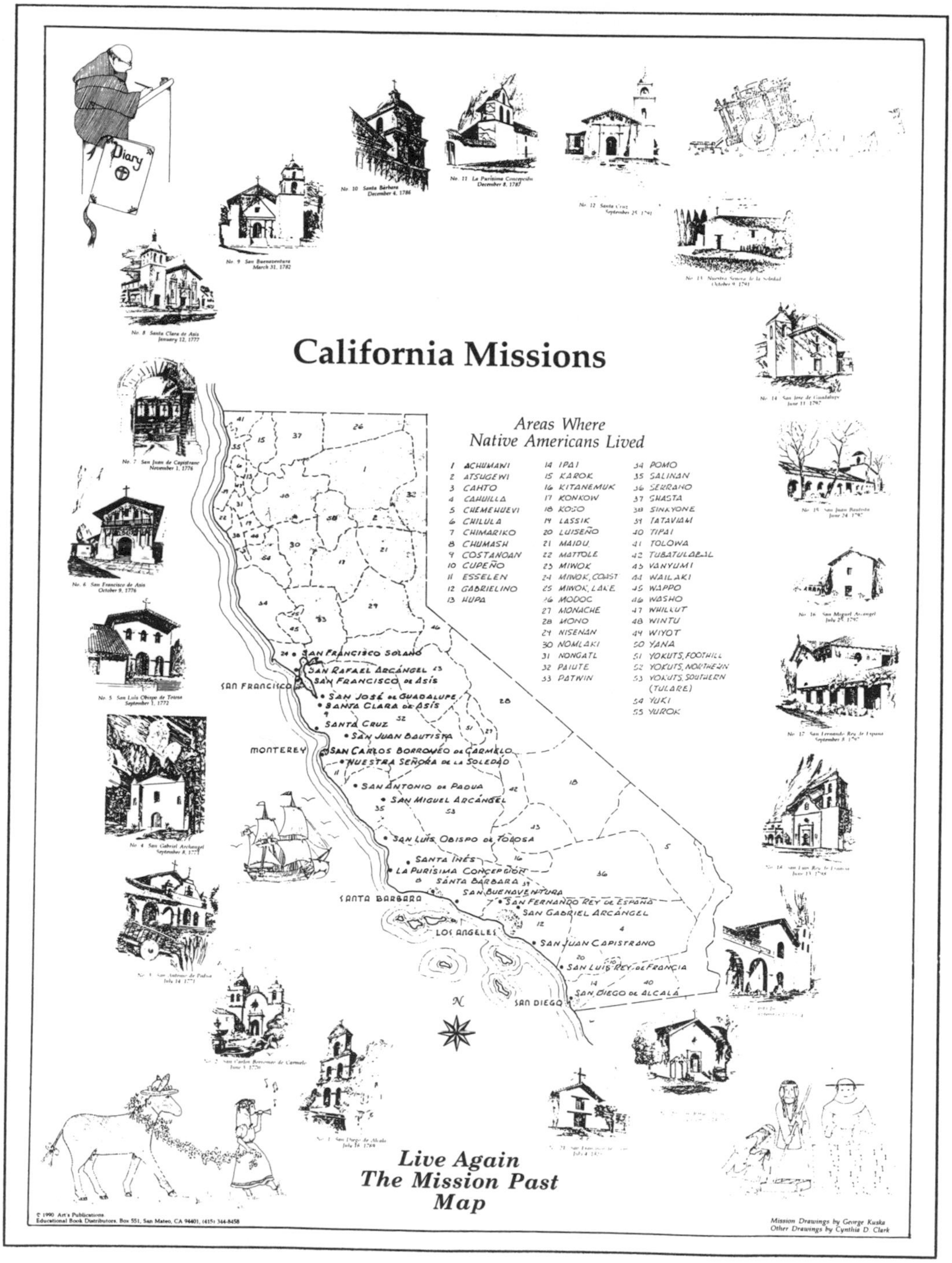